The Way To Happiness

The Way To Happiness

by

Iverna Tompkins

Logos International
Plainfield, New Jersey

All Scripture is taken from the King James Version of the Bible, unless otherwise noted.

Parenthetical Scripture locations in the text do not necessarily mean that the immediately preceding words are quoted from any particular version of the Bible, but that a similar thought occurs in that location.

To my co-worker, secretary, and
friend, Shirlee Green.

THE BEATITUDES

Blessed are the poor in spirit: for theirs is the kingdom of heaven.

Blessed are they that mourn: for they shall be comforted.

Blessed are the meek: for they shall inherit the earth.

Blessed are they which do hunger and thirst after righteousness: for they shall be filled.

Blessed are the merciful: for they shall obtain mercy.

Blessed are the pure in heart: for they shall see God.

Blessed are the peacemakers: for they shall be called the children of God.

Blessed are they which are persecuted for righteousness' sake: for theirs is the kingdom of heaven.

Blessed are ye, when men shall revile you, and persecute you, and shall say all manner of evil against you falsely, for my sake.

Rejoice, and be exceeding glad: for great is your reward in heaven: for so persecuted they the prophets which were before you.

(Matt. 5:3-12)

CONTENTS

Introduction

The "blessed are ye's ..." that form the opening statements of Christ's challenging Sermon on the Mount have charmed the Christians, challenged the religionists, and comforted the godly for hundreds of years. They have served as fodder for thousands of sermons, and are a memorization "must" for Sunday school students. They read like unrhymed poetry, but they carry the aura of unfathomable philosophy. They are unquestionably beautiful, but their beauty is the kind with a bite. They go against the grain of common sense by seeming to extol weakness and teaching that virtue is a value in its own right that will eventually conquer all evil and inherit the earth.

Many readers have approached this passage as so much "pie in the sky bye and bye," dismissing the Beatitudes as being too impractical for our modern generation.

Others like to emphasize that these are the "*be* attitudes" that tell us what we should be. These Bible students try to model their inner lives according to these rules of action.

Some expositors have pointed out that the Beatitudes are the bylaws of the church that Christ was forming. These teachers handle the Sermon on the Mount much as a trial lawyer handles statute law—as so much ammunition in their arsenal of weapons.

But Iverna Tompkins sees these hallowed exhortations as more than precious promises, admirable admonitions, or legal legacies. She views these beautiful beatitudes as practical principles at work in Christ's present kingdom on this earth in the here and now.

When the Spirit began to unfold these great truths to my sister some years ago, she was co-pastoring with me in a church on the West Coast. During successive morning services she electrified our congregation with this series of messages, and the fruit of that teaching ripened for years in the lives of many who sat under her ministry.

Little did either of us know at that time that each would be given to the entire body of Christ as traveling teachers. Again and again Iverna has shared this series—enlarging on certain portions, condensing others, polishing the whole, and enhancing the message with every change.

Now this fountainhead of truth is available to us in printed form. I commend it to you fully, certain of the excitement and enthusiasm you will feel as you read this helpful book. If these principles get ahold of your life you will join a host of others who have been changed for the better through Iverna's versatile and valuable ministry.

Judson Cornwall

The Way
To Happiness

CHAPTER ONE

Looking for Happiness

As I travel around I watch people. In shopping centers and other public buildings I notice people elbowing their way through crowds and cramming together at sales, dragging their kids along while the children want to go in several different directions at once. Surely this is not what life's all about!

I've observed the same type of confusion with regard to the desire for happiness. I don't need to give you statistics on how many millions of dollars are spent every year in a futile attempt to fulfill the quest for happiness. Recreation facilities are being built at a rapid pace and everybody is trying to find peace. People are looking for happiness. They're hunting for joy.

I have a theory—it is not a doctrine—that every individual possesses an innate desire and ability to worship. This is proven to us by the heathen who, when they have no god, create one. They make their own god out of something material, set it up and say, "That is our god!" And they begin to worship it.

Until the individual develops a desire to worship the true and living God there will always be a quest, a hunting, a looking, a searching, a seeking. God has so made us—spirit, soul and body. We have been created in His image.

In the world today men and women have reversed this divine order. In our society the body is in control. For one thing, we're hearing a lot of teaching about the body—the body must have this much recreation, and you must do certain exercises to keep the body in shape. As the apostle Paul points out, there is some profit in bodily exercise but the problem comes when we overemphasize this.

The soul is the seat of the intellect and the emotions. The body is seeking sexual gratification, and in response to this, we see pornography and filth all around us. "He which is filthy, let him be filthy still" (Rev. 22:11). Are you seeing the truth of this Scripture in the world today? What was filthy five years ago doesn't look so dirty today. It's a progressive thing. And people in the world are confused—so, whatever the body wants, the soul thirsts for.

A person who is motivated by the needs and wants of the body above everything else cannot come to an understanding of the cry, "My soul thirsteth for God, for the living God." Because the body is in control and the soul is thirsting for excitement and sensuality and promotion and possessions and fame, it is unable to cry for God.

Everyone has the potential for spiritual thirst, but this can only be realized as the individual reverses his priorities to put spirit first, then soul, then body. Psalm 23 tells us, "He restores my soul." Now how does the soul get restored? We have spirit, soul and body. When the body is in charge, the soul demands whatever the body wants. Only an unholy spirit is comfortable in that environment.

When Jesus becomes Lord in a life, however, the person ceases to be ego-centered. Instead, he becomes Christ-centered, and the Holy Spirit comes into the individual's spirit. The Holy Spirit enters the very nature of mankind. When the Holy Spirit comes into my spirit He becomes the star. He's in control. Now my soul can't go in the former directions, it goes in God's direction. And, therefore, my soul is restored.

Rest and restoration come to my soul, and I say, "My soul thirsteth for God." When a person is rightly related to God, filled with the Holy Spirit, his spirit and soul are thirsting for God, for His Word, for His ways, for His purposes. Then he doesn't have the problems with the body that had occupied such a great portion of his thought life and consideration previously.

The body isn't that important! It needs to be controlled but if we make it the focal point of our lives, we are diverted from truth. Paul explained that we're not ignorant of the enemy's devices, but I don't know that we can say this in the same way as Paul. I think we're *very* ignorant of Satan's devices and tactics even though he hasn't used anything new for a long time. He doesn't have to! What he has always used continues to work.

The enemy has three specific tactics. The first one is *denial*. Anytime you get anything from God, the enemy will do everything he can to get you to deny it. Have you ever been in a meeting where God has blessed and delighted you with His presence and you barely got out when doubts came into your mind? You begin to say, "Oh, I got caught up in the emotion of it and. . . ." Well, that's the tactic of the enemy. He attempts to get you to deny what has happened.

If that doesn't work, his second attempt will

be *acceleration.* If he can get you to go to an extreme in a thing, do it too much, focus too heavily on it, he's gotten you into error just as cleverly as he got you to deny it. You need only walk into a bookstore to discover some of the extreme teachings that are being advanced. You will find that such teachings all have an element of truth in them. There has been truth in every religion that has come up against the Word of God. There is always enough truth to make it believable, and usually enough Scripture to substantiate it. That's what happened with Mormonism, Christian Science, etc. A little bit of truth got accelerated in those directions, and the enemy said, "If it's good, then go, go, go. . . ."

You can get people to do all kinds of very funny things to lose their witness and testimony to the world. I think the days are behind us in which we need to be weird to be seen. Some of us grew up during an era when we had to look different and act strange in order for people to know we were Christians. Well, it's true that they knew we were Christians, but they found no pleasure in being around us and they certainly didn't want anything we had to offer even though they could easily point out who we were! Thank God, those days are behind us and I believe now we're becoming aware that the true witness of the believer is what brother Peter said, "Be ready always to give an answer to every man that asketh you a reason of the hope that is in you" (1 Pet. 3:15). In other words, your life style is going to cause people to question, "Why are you at peace? Why are you at rest? How can you be so joyful? Don't you understand the problems of the world?" Such questions become our opportunity to tell them of Jesus' life within us.

So the first attempt of the enemy is denial, the second is acceleration, and the third is as clever as the first two. It is *diversion*. If you go one degree off your course long enough you eventually become miles away from your destination. Either we have seen more of this in recent times or I have simply become increasingly aware of it. As the truth is just diverted one degree, people are being carried off into extremes of all kinds. *Overemphasized truth is error.* We need to be as "wise as serpents and as harmless as doves." That's the call of a disciple, according to our Lord (Matt. 10:16). Wisdom comes in part from understanding the devices of the enemy.

We cannot be idealistic, we cannot be super-spiritual in our attitudes and still help men and women who are right here living today. This Christian walk is reality in the here and now. It's a real life in which we're living. We used to believe you got saved and baptized and filled with the Holy Spirit in order to

endure to the end. In fact, our testimonies used
to go like that: "I just thank the Lord for saving
me and keeping me; I pray that I will hold on
to the end." Isn't that tragic? I heard one
minister say, "If I believed that, I'd get people
saved, baptized, filled with the Spirit and then
shoot them."

We're trying to help men, women, young
people and even boys and girls discover the
kingdom life today. Jesus said that the
kingdom of heaven is at hand. Those were the
opening words of His ministry. He told people
to repent or change their minds for the
kingdom of heaven is *now*. For years we didn't
see this, but thank God we're seeing it today.

Scripture must always be interpreted in the
light of Scripture. We don't pull one Scripture
verse out and build a doctrine around it.
Another way to interpret Scripture is to look at
it in the light of its setting or context—where it
is located. What happened before the
particular passage and what happened
afterwards? It is also necessary to understand
to whom it was written and for what purpose.

CHAPTER TWO

Becoming Poor in Spirit

BLESSED ARE THE POOR IN SPIRIT:
FOR THEIRS IS THE KINGDOM OF
HEAVEN. (Matt. 5:3)

The way to happiness as Jesus taught it is
revealed in the Sermon on the Mount (Matt. 5).
This beneficial passage of Scripture contains
the Beatitudes—"the attitudes we are to be."

Just prior to Jesus' teaching here He had
gone calling His disciples unto himself. "Follow
me, and I will make you to become fishers of
men" (Matt. 4:19). *"Follow me, follow me,"* and as
He went about calling His disciples, the
multitudes became aware of His presence and
they came to Him. At that time His blood had
not been shed, but they saw the reality of God
in Him. And so they came. How did they come?
They came sick, they came burdened, they

came distressed, they came possessed, they came just as they were. We know that because just prior to this passage it says, "And he healed them" (Matt. 4:24).

I think it's very important that we understand these steps. Sometimes we work backwards with people. We try to teach them a truth that has just become real to us. And it's like leading a blind man through an art gallery. They have no comprehension of what we are saying at all.

Once I was privileged to be on the very mountain where Jesus taught—the Mount of Beatitudes. It is located in a gorgeous area and it provides a very natural setting for teaching. It is a rolling hill and I could see how it provides a natural arena where people gathered from all three sides and obviously they were able to hear the Master well.

After Jesus called them, after He healed them, the Bible says, "Seeing the multitudes, he went up into a mountain . . ." (Matt. 5:1). He did not ascend the hill to escape the people, but He went up there so He could teach them. His disciples came to Him and there is every indication that they gathered close around Him. Some teach that the Beatitudes were for the disciples only, but I cannot conceive of the multitude suddenly dispersing when Jesus sat down to teach. They wanted to be a part of it too.

There was a mixed multitude present during the Sermon on the Mount. There were the disciples, the followers, the curiosity seekers, the Sadducees (who didn't believe in the eternal soul), the Herodians (who held to a political-religious belief), and the Separatists (who lived off in monasteries and little groups unto themselves). All of them came to hear Him.

Jesus began to teach, knowing that there were many present who had only come to see a miracle. I see the same phenomenon taking place today. I meet many people who are not content any longer in a local church or place of teaching. They just want miracles, and they're running to this place and that place looking for them. Do you know that miracles are for babies? Just to see a miracle is for a baby! That's because miracles are milk, not strong meat. It's fine if you want a glass of milk once in a while, but don't live on milk; we have to learn to eat a balanced diet and that is part of what a local church can provide.

While I was in Detroit some time ago, a young school teacher came to the Lord. As I was counseling and praying with her after the service, I told her that the important thing is for her to stay with God's people. I asked her, "Do you have a local church?"

Her answer shocked me! She said, "This is the first time in my life I have ever been with God's people." She must have been twenty-eight to thirty years of age. "The first time in my life I have ever been with God's people!" You see, we can't take for granted that people have the same background we have.

I grew up in church. My daddy was my pastor. And so it's hard for me to think a person could live twenty-five or so years and never be with God's people. This young lady had undoubtedly ridden buses and worked alongside believers and never knew it until one of her fellow teachers invited her to come to a meeting. And there she was beautifully born into the family of God.

If the body had communicated with this woman and caused her to become aware of the truth, perhaps she would have been born again earlier. Then she would have been nourished with what would have given her a good foundation in the things of God for which she eventually developed such a great desire.

Is it possible we're too busy running from meeting to meeting beholding the miraculous to realize not only our own need of proper spiritual food, but the need of encouraging others as well?

Many newborn Christians are being encouraged by people who have known the

Lord for many years to attend all kinds of special meetings with them. Very seldom do these young Christians become aware of their need to eat spiritual food regularly on their own. Whether miracles are appetizers or desserts, I'm not sure, but either way they're not meat and potatoes.

There's not anything more important today than getting into the Word of God and knowing what it says. I'm excited by miracles. Please don't misunderstand me and say, "She doesn't believe in healings and the supernatural." I do believe in those blessings and I've been a recipient of many miracles, but I have learned that the thing that sustains the joy of my life is the Word of God.

"The joy of the Lord is your strength." We love to sing that. We love to talk about it. But few people realize where that comes from. It's found in the book of Nehemiah (8:10). Do you know why it was stated this way? It was because the people had not had God's Word for years. When it was rediscovered, the people were brought together and they stood in reverence for hours while the Word was read to them. The Word of God so pricked their spirits that they began to weep and mourn over the realization that *they had not been true to God's Word*. After a period of weeping and mourning their leaders stood up and said, "Go your way, eat the fat, and drink the sweet, and send portions unto them for whom nothing is prepared: for this day is holy unto our Lord: neither be ye sorry; for the joy of the Lord is your strength" (Neh. 8:10). In other words, "Dry your tears, we're going to have a feast now. It's time for us to rejoice. There's a time to weep and there's a time to laugh. The joy of the Lord is your strength." So you cannot separate joy from the Word of God. And until men and women and young people are brought back to the Word of God, instead of the interpretation of the Word, there will be an absence of true joy.

The Scripture is of no private interpretation. To just hear sermons and messages and see programs and listen to tapes and read books is not enough. We must come back to the Word of God and let the Holy Spirit, who indwells the life of every believer, speak to us. The Holy Spirit makes the Word come alive to our hearts. That's why I continually emphasize the necessity for getting into the Word and understanding it.

Jesus began his dissertation on the mount with the word "blessed" (Gr., *makarios*). "Blessed are the poor in spirit: for theirs is the kingdom of heaven." The word "blessed" means "happy." Happy—in a blissful state!

The word "gospel" means "good news." So

when we share with others, we don't start with, "You know you are damned and you're a sinner and you're on your way to hell!" We're not selling fire insurance! We are selling, if you will, happiness, joy, peace, righteousness, kingdom living. "Righteousness, and peace and joy in the Holy Ghost" (Rom. 14:17). And so we can say to others, "Let's look at what Jesus said."

Jesus said, "In an enviable position—happy, completely fulfilled— is the individual who is poor in spirit." Now what does this mean? The Greek word for man's spirit is *pneuma*. Man's spirit is the rational part of him. The soul is the whole excitable self part. Have you ever gotten your spirit riled up? Have you ever wanted to get somewhere when the car ahead of you wanted to get there more slowly than you? We have a little horn that helps people know our position sometimes. From time to time this spirit of mine wants to rise up and demand some things. Jesus said, "Blessed are the poor, the wanting in spirit." This verse speaks to us of genuine humility.

I really have a problem with the way humility is being taught in some circles today. It is suggested that humility means possessing nothing, owning nothing, not looking like you are a child of the King but looking destitute and needy, and not claiming any rights to anything.

And that is humility. I don't think so; I think it's simply being poor. And I'm not at all sure, unless the Lord would lead someone that way, that He gets a great deal of glory out of such a scene.

Jesus did say how hard it is for the rich to enter the kingdom, and this is true, but He didn't say it is impossible, did He? With man it may seem impossible, but with God nothing is impossible.

The whole of our lives is made up very simply. It's like this: there is the self and there is the super-self. The whole purpose of the super-ego is to protect the ego, even if it has to lie.

You say something about me that is true but it hurts. You say, "She needs to lose weight." I don't want to hear that, so I get a break in my ego instantly. I'm hurt. You hurt my feelings. My superego has a job now because the ego has a crack in it. So my superego says, "Wow! Big deal! So does he!" See? And it begins to fill in its crack. "You're not fat; you're pleasingly plump." The superego will say anything to heal the ego.

Now when the Holy Spirit comes into our spirits, the superego becomes possessed by Him, and the whole purpose is conviction and this is never a lasting thing. Condemnation lasts and destroys, but conviction is always for the purpose of correction. That's why in the mercy of God, He will first convict and then withdraw. Have you known that in your own life? The Holy Spirit zeroes in on something until you think you're going to die. But you refuse to die; you refuse to give the thing up. The Holy Spirit moves off and lets you survive.

Condemnation does not come from God. Do you know that? In the end time condemnation will come from God. That's the end-time punishment or the result of the wages of sin. But not now. Condemnation comes from the enemy. You can't get rid of condemnation. "You're guilty, you're guilty, you're guilty; I tell you, you'll never make it!" *That's from the enemy*.

The Bible says that all we need to do is submit ourselves unto God. We resist the devil by submitting to God. And because he can't stay when we're in that situation, he runs from us (James 4:7).

But humility is real. Even though it's been taught to an extreme, that does not take away the real. It's a sad thing for us to throw out the real just because we become aware of the counterfeit! There are many counterfeits in the body of Christ but I'm not going to throw out the genuine just because the enemy made up a fake one.

"Blessed are the poor in spirit." I had a long-distance talk with a lady who had a problem in her relationship with another Christian woman. She said the other lady had hurt her in a very real way. In fact, she was contemplating filing a suit for defamation of character against the other woman. Now what's wrong with her? Does she know the Lord? Yes, she does. Is she filled with the Holy Spirit? Yes, she is! What's wrong with her then—that she would take a sister in Christ to court and sue her? The problem is that she's not poor in spirit! She's rich in her own spirit, not the Spirit of God. And she's determined to take care of the other lady no matter what!

Now I can certainly understand those feelings. When I first learned to drive, I read the driver's manual through and I learned what all of my rights were. If I would come to an intersection and was one inch into the intersection and an approaching car was not, I would take my right. And my poor father, who was teaching me how to drive, would say, "Honey, now you came awful close."

And I would say, "But I had the right of way!"

One day, my father, who was a very quiet man, said, "I shall make sure that is your epitaph: 'My daughter had the right of way.'"

You know, I must be willing to get rid of that word, "right"! "I have a right!" How many of you know that you have the right to a lot of things, but the Spirit of the Lord says, "Let it go! Let it go! I'll deal with it." What's so wrong about me protecting me? Only one thing, if I do it, He won't. The Lord is my defense—and He does so much better than I do. He has a way of defending me without injuring the other person.

God has a way of killing enemies. Do you know how He does it? He makes them become our friends. Isn't that a delightful way to get rid of all our enemies? "Lord, tramp them down, mash them." Have you ever identified with David's Psalms when he was a little upset with his enemy? "Lord, get 'em! Tramp them down."

The Lord says, "I will, but it will be my way! My ways are not your ways." And He just begins to draw them in His love and grace. And pretty soon my enemy is my brother! My enemy is my sister and I find her coming to me and saying, "Oh, sister, I have not always understood you, but I have such a love for you."

I pray, "Lord, you do things in such strange ways!"

He answers, "Yes, my ways are higher than your ways." So, "Blessed are the poor in spirit."

Have you ever found somebody who is happy rushing through life seeking only his rights? I never have. I said to the lady who was going to sue her former friend, "The only thing I have to say to you is: If you win the suit you will lose." And we began to talk about the Lord being our defense.

Why does God let us go through some things? That He might break down our spirits! Some of us, by virtue of our backgrounds and the way we were raised, have felt that we have to set up defenses to protect us so we can live. I had two younger brothers and two older brothers, but no sisters. I set up certain defenses against being the only girl. Whenever they went seven steps up the ladder, I would go eight and I have a scar to prove it. Anything they could do, I could do. Do you know what that did to me as a woman? It made me extremely competitive. I competed with men.

Needless to say, I wasn't the most ideal wife in the world either. If you're curious enough, you can read my book, *How to Be Happy in No Man's Land*. I was backslidden, away from God, and married to a man who didn't know the Lord, but I don't really place the blame on that. I was simply an aggressive, defensive, competitive woman. And when you put those three adjectives together in one woman, I don't think even God can live with it. Then the Lord permitted me to get myself involved in situations designed to break my spirit. Many of you are familiar with an old hymn we used to sing, "My stubborn will at last hath yielded. I would be thine, and thine alone."

We begin to realize that we are failures. That's a devastating realization for someone who has been rich in his own spirit. "I can do it myself. I know this, and I know that." I was successful in everything I did and in every direction of my work and I made lots of money and so on. Unhappy, wanting, longing, aching, wrongly related until finally I was completely stripped of everything I ever owned. I made an investment and overnight everything was taken from me. My home, my car, my bank account. They repossessed everything but the kids. And I tell you for someone who is full of his own spirit and pride, that was a hard thing. I went through depression.

Don't ever come against somebody and say that he's demon possessed if he's only depressed. Depression is a natural reaction to feelings of devastation. It can be dealt with by the Holy Spirit of God. Sometimes it is satanic, and in this case I wish it had been because I could have simply cast it out and gotten free. But, instead, I had to learn the truth of Isaiah 61:3. I had to learn about that wonderful divine exchange. "I'll give you beauty for ashes. Oil of joy for mourning. I'll give you the garment of praise in exchange for a spirit of heaviness." It's a difficult thing to give Him your ashes, and it's a difficult thing to give up the heaviness and the depression you feel. But once I made that commitment to Him, He kept His promise. I became aware of the simple truth that I don't have to compete with anyone. And that's an important fact.

A competitive spirit can be the beginning of attitudes which ultimately become depressive, but you don't have to compete with anyone. I am me. And you are you. We are uniquely called and chosen and ordained of God. Why He wanted each of us we may never know, but that He wanted us we *do* know.

I remember when I first started in the ministry. How would you like to grow up and learn how to minister in Judson Cornwall's church? If you've ever heard him you know what an articulate speaker he is and here I was assisting him in the music and youth departments, etc. I wasn't preaching or teaching and then one day he said, "You're going to have the night service." I almost had a heart attack. By then I had learned submission and there was nothing to do but to say, "Yes, sir!" It was a terribly frightening prospect!

Do you know the hardest part of my first two years of ministry? I wanted to be like Judson! I longed for that. I used to be thrilled with his teaching. I used to see hundreds of people who were simply exhilarated by his teaching. I noticed their response to the very precise and exact method of teaching he employs. He makes things so clear and when he gets through speaking, you have a definite outline. But I'd come across as if I were just saying, "Blah, blah." Oh, I would have loved to be like him.

I was afraid every time I'd go to minister. One day I was in prayer and I said, "Lord, I don't know why it is I'm always scared. My brothers are never scared. I've got three preacher brothers and they'd rather preach than eat. Lord, I wish you would do something with me."

And the Lord said, "I will when you stop competing."

And I answered, "Oh, Lord, I'm not competing. I know they're more wonderful than me."

Do you see what I'm saying? That's proof right there that I had set being like my brother as my goal. I have finally come to realize this, and it's taken several years for the Lord to get me from there to here. But finally I've learned that I can't be anybody else. Like it or leave it, I'm just what I am. Just as I am, the only plea I have is the blood of Jesus Christ. When you see that in your own life you will become poor in spirit.

When you see that you're poor or broken—broken into pieces, poor, shattered—then those pieces or the tangled strands of your life will be put together into a beautiful tapestry. You're going to find that when you've made Him Lord completely of your life there is joy and victory and peace and you're going to be able to look in the mirror and say, "Hello, I like you!" This is because He miraculously brings peace to our whole lives.

Jesus said, "Blessed are the poor in spirit for theirs is the kingdom of heaven." When is the kingdom? Oh, that's some day when Jesus— Oh, no, it's *now!* But the kingdom is only known by those who recognize the King. You can sing it, you can say it, but until you know that He is your Lord, you're not in the kingdom. "*He is Lord!*" We love to sing that. "He is Lord! He is risen from the dead and He is Lord. Every knee shall bow. . . ." That's good, that's true; many unwilling knees shall bow, for the Holy Spirit shall release the socket that holds them up and they'll bow. And the tongues will begin to confess Jesus Christ is Lord! Jesus Christ is Lord indeed! And for many who become aware of it, it will be too late. Every multitude will be shouting, "He is Lord!" Today is the day when the ear of God is tuned to hear the cry of His people, "He is Lord, He is Lord!"

You've done what you could with your life and it hasn't really turned out the way you wanted it to. So many times I have made resolutions and promises and gone forward in meetings and made commitments to the Lord. Haven't you? Perhaps you made a vow to God when you were in your teens and promised Him you'd go to Africa, China or some other foreign mission field. But since then you've married and have a family and there is no way you can keep that vow. Now that is a sin, but it's not unpardonable if you take it to the cross. Simply tell the Lord you promised Him something you could never fulfill. Let Him know that you are willing to obey Him in all things. Ask Him to make you sensitive from this time on. The important thing is that we make Him Lord of our lives. "King of my life I crown Thee now—Thine shall the glory be; Lest I forget Thy thorn-crowned brow, Lead me to Calvary." That's the only place where I can recognize any good in me. I see the crown on His head. I become aware that He died for me.

Jesus speaks: "I died to pick up the tangled strands of your life. I died to shape you as a lump of clay over and over and over and over."

"How many times, Lord?"

"Until you can hold the oil and wine that comes from Zion. Blessed are the poor in spirit: for theirs is the kingdom of heaven."

CHAPTER THREE

Mourning

BLESSED ARE THEY THAT MOURN:
FOR THEY SHALL BE COMFORTED.
(Matt. 5:4)

In the previous chapter we have established
that we must want to be poor in spirit.
Sometimes, though, we get so humble that we
become proud of our humility. The Bible says,
"Blessed are the poor in spirit. . . ." This is
literally translated to mean, "In a state of bliss,
in a state of happiness is the individual who is
poor in his own spirit." From this statement we
can infer that such an individual is rich in the
Lord's Spirit if he is poor in his own spirit.

In my spirit I am possessed by the Holy
Spirit. We need to tell people who are seeking
the baptism in the Holy Spirit that they are
seeking to be possessed by Him. They really
are. And when that possession takes place,
things change from that point on.

Have you ever noticed that someone with an unholy spirit suddenly is not comfortable around you? I have a classic example of that. I got on a 747 flight to Hawaii; I had my secretary-companion with me at that time and the seats we were given were taken so they reassigned us. We had just gotten comfortably located when passengers came to claim our seats. It was takeoff time by then and the plane was filled so the flight attendant came and said, "Don't feel badly, girls; I'll put you in the lounge."

I suppose nine out of ten people would have been very thrilled with that promotion, but we weren't too happy with it. Anyway, we went into the lounge—it was a very lovely room, with tables in the middle and chairs that swivel. The bar was on the right when we walked in so we walked over to the left thinking perhaps we would be by ourselves a little bit. There was a booth with some gals in it. They said, "Come on over here and we'll have a good time."

"No, we'll just stay here," we replied. Then a lady came into the lounge. She was a "blonde bomber." She took a quick sweep around the room. In my mind she was looking to see how the pickings were! She looked at us and went on and then she came right back and looked at me as if she knew me. And I thought, "Hello?" She came over and sat down in a chair across from me and just glared at me with hate looks. I knew that this little, fat, graying mama wasn't a threat to the "blonde bomber." She couldn't be angry with me personally, and I didn't know what the problem was. Every time anyone came into the lounge, she would get up and go over to talk with them. Then she would point back at me and they would all laugh. Now for about the first five or ten minutes of this, I was very strong in the Lord. But after a while I wanted to smear her. The desire was very strong to go to her and ask what she was saying. But I thought I couldn't handle it. This went on for hours. Finally, someone reported it and the flight attendant came and asked me if I was having a problem. I reported, "Well, I think *she's* having the problem but I don't know what it's all about."

He explained, "I don't have any place to move you—I'm so sorry. I think she's high on something."

I kept trying to ignore her and we turned our chairs away from her, but she kept moving so she could keep looking at us. I don't know why it took me so long to discover that I wasn't dealing with a *person*, but with a *spirit*. It came to me clearly—"You're not dealing with a woman, you're dealing with a spirit."

By this time, she was talking with a group of people again and they were laughing as she kept pointing toward me; I looked over and when this revelation hit me I said, "I bind you, spirit, in the name of Jesus." And when I did, she dropped her head and never bothered me the rest of the time. She never even looked my way.

This story makes the point. It's the poorness of my own spirit that counts. There was a day when I would have gone directly to the woman and had a verbal confrontation with her. "What is it with you?" It is in our own spirits that the Holy Spirit dwells. If we defend ourselves, He will not be our defense. I promise this to you on the authority of God's Word. Do you want to be your own defense? Go ahead, and good luck, because God won't defend you while you're defending you. If you want the advocate with the Father, Jesus Christ the righteous, to plead your case (1 John 2:1), then you have to step out of your own defensive position and let Him represent you in the confrontation that's taking place.

"Blessed are they that mourn: for they shall be comforted." The word "mourn" is *pentheo* in the Greek, and it literally means "to lament for." The same word is used in Luke 23:27 when it refers to the followers of Jesus. As Jesus was being led away to be crucified, a great company of people followed Him which also bewailed and lamented Him. Now this is speaking of sorrow. The same word is used in the book of Acts in reference to those who felt badly about Stephen when he was stoned. Acts 8:2 says, "Devout men carried Stephen to his burial, and made great lamentation over him." This is speaking of natural mourning.

Mourning is not wrong. In some Christian circles people seem to have the idea that they must have a super-spiritual approach to mourning. For example, I was called to share with a minister in a funeral for one of his parishioners. The deceased had been in the ministry for many years and his wife was sitting in the front of the church. The pastor poked me and told me to look at the widow. He said, "That is beautiful to me; do you see her?" I looked down at her and saw on her face a kind of pastey smile that was obviously forced. He said, "We had a talk with her that the Christian does not mourn the loss of a loved one because we have a hope laid up for us in heaven." This is a picture of diversion from truth. We do not mourn as the world mourns; that is a fact, a Christian truth. We do not mourn as though we have no hope, and that is a fact. However, we *do* mourn for *our* sakes. Grief and mourning are purposeful. They are God's vehicles to get us from one point to the next—from despair to hope.

Let me give you nine steps which are

common to the process of grief and mourning. The first is *shock*—even if the individual has been terminally ill for a long time, no one is ever really prepared for death. No matter how prepared to face it we feel, when the death of a loved one occurs, we are shocked! By nature we are not able to handle this kind of thing. Grief is not limited to death. We can grieve over failure. You will find people grieving over defeat in their lives, the plans and goals they did not attain. People genuinely grieve over promotions they felt they earned and didn't receive. There are parents grieving over youngsters who are living beneath the standards they had been taught. Broken homes cause grief. The loss of a loved one in the form of a broken engagement or other separation can cause deep-seated grief in people. We must not minimize it.

Remember this, grief is related to the age of the individual. What's important to me at forty-seven is not the same thing that bothered me at twenty-seven. And what bothered me at twenty-seven looks so superficial to me today. I would have to work at feeling badly over the same things now. So, no matter whether you're a teen-ager, a child or an adult, the first step a person experiences is that of shock.

The second step is *expression*. Crying is the

most normal way to express grief. But please remember when I tell you it is not the only way. In our society it's often difficult for men to cry. We teach them from the time they're little boys that men don't cry. How many times have you heard a mother say, when a boy comes in with a crushed finger, "Come on now, big men don't cry!"? Now that's bad and may God help us and change us from raising boys in that negative way.

When I've been in Israel, it has been a delight to see the lack of inhibitions men have there. If they feel like crying, they just bawl all over each other. I love it. It is this kind of tenderness that I miss in American men. I've learned that American men feel just as tender, but they have often been taught the importance of maintaining a facade, an exterior front that says, "I'm a man; me male, me no cry." And so, men often push all these emotions down deep inside. But, they need to have some kind of expression.

Even some women, by virtue of external pressures, have developed defense mechanisms whereby they don't cry. There was a time in my life after my marriage had failed, and I had been hurt in many different ways, that I cried and cried and cried. I'm sure I hurt others also, but I'm telling you this from my point of view. Have you ever cried until you were sick of crying? I felt like a human waterfall and I made up my mind that I was not going to cry another tear. Zap! For five full years I never shed a tear. It became increasingly difficult to pray because I didn't let any tenderness develop. It was almost impossible for anyone to get to know me. I just gave them what I wanted them to have. I doled myself out in pieces. Someone may have known me as a teacher and another as a musician, but every person could know me only by whatever I let them see.

One day I was standing on the beach, looking over the ocean with a lady friend of mine throwing rocks into the surf like little kids. We were having a good time doing this, but suddenly she reached down, picked up a pebble and handed it to me. "Here," she challenged. "Whenever you decide to tumble your wall I'd like very much to be the first inside." I felt like pushing her in; she was so right on. Instead of throwing the rock, for some reason that I now know was the Lord, I put it in the coin purse of my wallet and every time I opened that purse, there was that dumb rock and it would "speak" to me. "When are you going to let someone break through your wall?"

I would always answer, "I have no walls!"

I have a little cartoon book that I appreciate so much. It is called *The Facade*. You know what

34

a facade is, don't you? It's the exterior we put on for others to see. One of my favorite cartoons in the book shows a man standing behind his own image which he's holding up. It has a little hole right in the center, and he's calling out through the hole, "There's no hole!" Point is well made, isn't it? We do have our facades. The Lord was able to help me break down my walls, and He will help you with yours.

We must permit people to express their grief in whatever ways they can. Some people will have to withdraw. They'll have to pull the shades and be alone. I know people who have been deeply hurt by well-meaning individuals who rush into the house of the grieving one with a crowd of people and a whole lot of food, saying, "You can't do this. Get the shades up—open up this place now." There's a time for that, but first there must be an expression of feelings. Maybe they really need to just be left alone for a few days. Some people do. They can't all just cry. When my daddy died, we as a family rejoiced at his funeral and praised the Lord. We sang, "On Christ, the solid rock I stand." I'm sure the funeral attendants thought we were a bit balmy, but we just rejoiced in the Lord and had a good time. Mother had wept for mother; my brothers had wept for themselves, but I had not yet cried because I felt the need, as the only girl, to hold up for everyone else. Afterwards, mother went to the beach with a friend and my brothers. Then I went back to the family house to clear out dad's belongings, rearrange and do the things you do when there has been a death in the family. That was my time for letting down. My expression came as I was by myself all night long, cleaning my daddy's home, seeing the chair he had used and folding his clothes. It was ridiculous, if you look at it logically. It wasn't death for him—it was graduation. I know he's waiting and I'll spend eternity with him. My weeping wasn't for him; it was for me. *Me!* I missed him and I knew every time I'd go home from that point on, his chair would be empty. Dad wouldn't be there, so my grief was spilled in tears.

The third step is a feeling of *being depressed and lonely.* Loneliness is not related to people being around you. Oh, how I wish we really knew that. I have had some of my loneliest times in the midst of multitudes.

I remember one time when I was at Elim Bible Institute, speaking at a meeting and staying on campus. People would come by and say, "Oh, how are you doing?" The staff treated me like royalty. I had everything going for me. One afternoon, I stepped outside and, like a cold blanket of ice, loneliness hit me. I looked out at that campus—kids were switching from chapel to classes, masses of people were around and I knew that any person there would give me time or attention or anything else I would have asked for. Suddenly I was confronted by the thought, "You don't belong to anybody." It overwhelmed me! "You don't fit in with the staff; you don't fit in with the students; you're not married; you're not really single; you're nothing." That overwhelming sense of not belonging to anyone flooded my being. Unless you've experienced it, you honestly cannot understand. I went back to my room and held a "pity party" all alone. Poor me! I fluffed me a "pity pillow" and began to sob. Now that's all right, unless you stay there.

When you encounter this in people, and they say, "I just can't stop crying; I'm so all alone," it is not always wise counsel to say, "Well, get out and get with people." It is possible to have lots of people all around you and still feel very lonely. All we need to say to them is, "I know how you feel; there are times of loneliness in all our lives." There are even periods of loneliness in the lives of those who have their companions beside them too. There are times when a man and woman love each other dearly and deeply and sleep side by side yet still, one or the other has a great sense of being all alone. It's part of life, but it won't last forever.

The fourth step involves *physical symptoms*. When you are in a state of grief, pains may develop in parts of your body you didn't know you owned. Backaches, leg aches, arm aches, finger aches, muscle aches and all kinds of symptoms which are referred to as psychosomatic illnesses. Eighty-seven percent of the illnesses that come to the attention of the doctors today have been declared to be psychosomatic in nature. Isn't that shocking? Eighty-seven percent! Some people think that means they're pretended illnesses, but you need to learn that that's not true. A psychosomatic illness is just as much an illness as a physiological illness. It's not a fake thing because it takes on physical symptoms and if it is permitted to go on, it can literally take people to their deaths. It is not unreal. Psychosomatic illness means that because of an emotional problem we have become physically ill. This is very simplistic and nonclinical, but it may help you to understand what I'm trying to say.

There is one part of you that will not take an overload. You can carry too much and strain your arms, and thereby overload yourself and rip your back out of place and a lot of other things, but your mind will not permit an overload. It simply will not. If you continue to strain it and take on additional pressures, it will begin to mount up. The best description I know of this is the pressure cooker. You put it over the heat and the steam builds up and it begins to hiss. Then it's all right for a while, but pretty soon it builds up again. There's a device on the lid called a petcock which throws off a little steam at a time. This keeps the lid from blowing off. But just let the petcock get stuck or let the heat get turned up to a point at which the steam outbuilds the escape mechanism, and what happens? An explosion!

That's an accurate description of psychosomatic illness. When the pressure becomes greater than my release program there is a blow-up and very often the only way my superego will permit me to blow up is to do it physiologically. It's not as embarrassing to be physically sick as it is to burst out in tears. That can be the reason for much of our illness.

The fifth step is *panic*. Panic leads to despair. It's different from shock, in that shock is an amazingly stunning anesthetic, but panic is not an anesthetic at all. Panic is despair. Panic says, "What will I do? Where will I go? There's no hope for me; it's the end. I can't make it any more!" A tragic position!

Step number six is most often misunderstood by we who are not going through grief when we see the people who are, and that is *guilt*. People who go through grief inevitably come to step number six, and it goes like this: "It must be something I did. I must have caused this to come upon me. It must be God visiting my sins upon me."

Or it can go like this: "If only I had known I would just have had him a certain number of years, how differently I would have treated him." Guilt! The only way I know to help people in this is to tell them that God's chastisement is always corrective to his kids. God's punishment to the unbeliever is fatal but God never deals with His children in a fatal position. He always chastises to bring us out of a problem.

Only God has the power of life and death. In a death situation the bereaved one may remember: "But I once wished him dead." Let me tell you there are few people who have ever lived together over a period of years where one hasn't wished the other dead in a moment of anger and frustration. Such a wish is not all that unique! One time I said that in a meeting, and two women raced up to me afterwards and exclaimed, "That's not true!" And I said, "Then why are you so upset?"

But guilt is something you have to help people through. Parents will have guilt about their children. I talked with one parent whose daughter had been very promiscuous. She had gotten on drugs and so on. The night she was killed, she had been bar-hopping and it was a case of insidious murder. A brutal beating, sexual involvement and a bullet through the head had taken her life. You can't imagine the guilt her parents felt as a result of this. I saw them coming through the different steps of grief, but when they got to the guilt stage, problems in their own home began to develop. The father had been a drinker and so on and so on.

And I said to them, "My dear friends, the only thing I can say to you is don't try to justify your past behavior. It probably is true that the environment of your home was not what God intended it to be. But if God is limited to the environment of homes, in order to bring men and women unto himself, I want out right now." How many stories have you heard of a kid out of this very kind of environment where God reached down and called the young person sovereignly out and filled him with the Spirit and sent him out to be a minister? My God is not limited by home environments.

I had to preach that young girl's funeral. They asked, "What hope can you give us?" I said, "I can give you the hope that I watched that girl come to church year after year, even during the period surrounding the birth of her illegitimate child. I watched her bring that child to church. I know she knew enough that if she had a dying breath she was able to say, 'Jesus, you are the Lord.' 'The mercy of God is an ocean divine. A boundless and fathomless tide' and I dare to believe she launched out. Whether she did or not, only eternity will prove. But I'll tell you this, if she's in hell, she's not in hell because of *you*." I think we have taken on a sovereignty about ourselves that belongs solely to almighty God.

I've had people tell me, "If you don't preach the gospel there will be hundreds of people who will never meet the Lord." I reject that! If I don't preach the gospel, woe is *me*! Not woe is *them*. Do you understand that? God is not limited to me.

Step number seven involves *hostility and resentment*. This level of grief and mourning is usually expressed this way: "Why me? Why me? Why did this happen to our family? I can't understand why God permitted this! If God is so loving and if God is so good why would He let this happen?"

When people don't want to face the reality of life, they look for a way out and their cop-out questions are, "If God is God then why are millions starving in India? If God is God why did He let my mate be taken from me even after I told Him I'd serve Him? Why?"

Once when I was in Virginia Beach, we prayed for a little, five-year-old girl who had a brain tumor. She was in the hospital and we had special prayer during the morning service. There were about 300 people in the meeting and we all beseeched the throne of God on behalf of that little girl. Her folks had just returned to the Lord and were walking with Him. We all agreed, "God, we believe you for this." But by the time of the evening service, the little girl had passed away. You can imagine the reaction of the people—especially the young people. "We don't understand; we don't understand! When the family of God got together and prayed and agreed as touching this healing in the name of Jesus and we believed for that, why did the little girl die? Can you explain it?"

And I said, "Thank you for being honest. And I'll be just as honest with you." Yes, I could explain it; my God is sovereign. My God sees the end from the beginning; I don't. And many of the things I would pray for and hang on to with tenacity would be destruction. If I could see the end I would know that what happened to the little girl had a purpose. We must learn to get people back to a proper concept of the nature of almighty God. Who is God? He is sovereign, omniscient. He knows everything. That's who God is. He has all knowledge. That is why He named himself, "I am Alpha and Omega." He didn't just start something, make a lot of promises and then walk away. He says, "I have the whole beginning and ending in my hand. And while you see one half of my rainbow I want you to know it's actually a circle. I have the other half right there. I am always out to do my children good." If you've raised children, you'll understand that. At the time you lay a particular restriction down to them, you're the worst mother or father in the world in their eyes at that moment. But you're out to do them good, aren't you? That's why you lay down some restrictions and require deprivations of privileges, etc. So hostility and resentment set in.

It will aid us in leaving this step to remind ourselves that our heavenly Father is out to do us good. Someone has said that we will never know what has been a good day or a bad one until all the days of our lives have been gathered to count their worth.

And step number eight is a sense of *being able to return to usual activities,* and it usually is expressed like this:

If I could just change jobs. . . .
If I could just get out of this house. . . .
If I could just move to another territory. . . .
If I just didn't have to see anything familiar again. . . .

There's only one good thing about step number eight, and that is that it's the step before number nine. In this phase there is seemingly no door open to the grieving individual—no opportunity. But this word can be given: "You know, I'm glad you said that to me, because you are almost out of grief now. You are on the next to the last step."

In step number nine *hope is restored.* The psychological term for this is "regrouping." Now, I don't know if it will make sense to you or not, but I promise you it is the truth. People can go to bed at night on step number eight and wake up on step number nine. It is the most incredible and unexplainable thing that happens. I've been through this; I understand what I'm saying. You go to bed at night, wishing you could die yet too scared to ask God to do anything about it. You have faith to die but do not have faith to live, and you tell God all the reasons.

Many of us think prayer is giving God unknown information. Telling God all of the reasons I shouldn't live and then lying down and saying, "Lord Jesus, please don't let me wake up." But one morning I wake up with this attitude, "Well, let's get on with the program!" Now I don't pretend to understand how that works, but I do know it does, for I have seen it in hundreds of lives. I've counseled with people in all stages of grief and when they reach the

45

point of no hope, I say, "You're almost out! You may not believe me about this. I didn't believe anybody either, but you're going to wake up one morning and you're going to find your mind planning, 'Let's see now, it's ridiculous for me to think of leaving town—I have a job to do here.' " That's called regrouping.

There are two other types of mourning. There is *sorrow for sin.* This is spoken of in James 4:8-9: "Draw nigh to God, and he will draw nigh to you. Cleanse your hands, ye sinners; and purify your hearts, ye double minded. Be afflicted, and mourn, and weep: let your laughter be turned to mourning, and your joy to heaviness."

In the church today we have taken that process away from people. Somebody comes forward to accept Jesus as his personal Savior and he begins to weep and the first thing we do is rush up and try to do everything we can to get him to stop crying. We say, "Listen, you don't have to cry. Jesus loves you. He gave himself for you." And we talk the individual out of it. But this verse indicates that there *is* a time for him to weep. Let him cry, let him mourn.

My mother is a beautiful person; she is seventy-five years old. She remarried after dad "graduated" and she is doing a whale of a job. I'm

sure she'll outlive all her kids, and she's a great
woman of God. My mother did something
when she was raising us that I held against her
for a long time. I've told her this and why she
did it I guess I'll never understand. She would
give us a licking and then say, "You shut up or
I'll give you something to cry about!" Now I
believe in spanking children—it happens to be
scriptural—but she would spank us and then
say, "Now quit crying!" When I told her about it
she said, "Well, that's because if I didn't stop
you, you would have gone on forever." She's
probably right about that, but in my mind when
I think back, it seems an unfair thing to do,
because it did not allow for a time of mourning.

When the Holy Spirit comes into a life to
bring conviction of sin, there ought to be a time
of mourning. As you can tell, I don't believe in a
sign-the-card and pass-it-up and I'll-
meet-you-in-heaven philosophy. I think we
need to let people weep. And when they're
weeping, we need to help them know why
they're weeping. So I say to people, "That's
good, sir; I'm glad you're weeping. I'm proud
of you for letting that show because you're
evidencing a brokenness to God. You're saying,
'Yes, I'm so sorry. I see myself in the light of
your holiness, your righteousness and I'm so
sorry that I haven't listened to you before.' "
Now, that's real. You can begin to help them
out of it after they've had their time of crying

and mourning.

Then there's another less understood kind of mourning. That is your *sorrow for other people*. If you've never known this, you won't understand it even by my description of it. If you have known it, you will understand it. First, we dealt with natural sorrow, then we discussed sorrow for sin, now we're looking at intercessory prayer or mourning on behalf of another.

I believe we're going to have a renewing of compassion in the church of the Lord Jesus Christ. The best way I have to describe compassion is by coining a word: "co-passion." When I see you in the eyes of my Father I care about you just like He does. This is so different from the philosophy, "You be nice to me; I'll be nice to you," or "You invite me to dinner; I'll invite you to dinner." Human nature, isn't it? But when He, with His pounding heart, or as Paul said, "from the bowels"—from the womb of mankind—gives forth mercy, that is a picture of genuine compassion. When you care so much whether the person is sinning or hurting, when you care so much that it seems you can feel what they feel, you are coming into true intercession.

The word "empathy" has to do with genuine relating. Now I don't want to be just empathized with; I want true compassion to flow and, in that way, I can receive from Him through you. One time a situation came into my life that was very, very negative and there seemed to be nothing I could do about it. I didn't know who believed what about me. It was at this low point that a lady came up to me and put her arm around me and said, "I don't want to talk to you about what's going on. I want you to know this—I really feel what you feel." I tell you there wasn't a ministry that had come to me that was comparable to those simple little words: "I feel what you feel."

Years went by and I was going through another negative time in my life. I was going through a great sense of loss and I was fighting bitterness and many other resentments. I wasn't sure where I stood. Have you ever been there? You weren't sure where you stood with Christ and you weren't sure where you stood with the body of Christ?

As I was going through that time of uncertainty, Costa Deir came up to me at a camp meeting. I don't know if he even knew who I was—I must someday ask him. But he came up to me and said, "Sister, I know that you have had one year of hell on earth." I asked him, "How do you know?" I knew he knows my brother Judson, and I thought Jud had told him about my situation but that wasn't it. He said, "Sometimes I had physical hurts; other times I felt that my heart was literally going to break. I have felt with you for one solid year and I have been wakened in the night and gotten on my knees and sought God on your behalf." Nobody knew me. I hadn't traveled; I was the one who "stuck by the stuff" while Judson traveled. I was a nothing, except to God. He loved me enough to speak to one of His key men in my behalf. The Lord woke him in the night and put my face before him.

That experience made me want to worship Costa, if you know what I mean. I wanted to fall down at his feet and say, "Let's have a foot washing service. Oh, my brother, I will do anything for you."

And the Lord spoke to me, "I did that." And He brought this Scripture to my mind: "Simon [or Peter], behold, Satan hath desired to have you, that he may sift you as wheat: But I have prayed for thee, that thy faith fail not" (Luke 22:31-32). And Jesus spoke to me as I was standing there looking into Costa's eyes and He said, "That's how I pray for you—through my church."

I know what it is to pray for people I don't even know. That's true intercession and I have groaned and wept with words that could not come out. Thank God for the Holy Spirit and His language for He knows how to pray.

Sometimes when I can't pray—perhaps in a meeting—a brother's face or a sister's face will linger before me. Returning to my hotel room, I still see the individual; sometimes I waken in the night and the person's face is still there and I'll groan, "Oh, God!" Jesus said, "That's an enviable state."

How many of you know that while you are having labor pains you would hardly believe anyone who said, "I envy you"? While I am in the thrust of laborious effort to bring forth, it doesn't look very enviable and yet Jesus said, "Blessed are they that mourn." Why? Because they shall be comforted. Now let me give you an understanding of this word. "Comforted" does not mean "released." If it did, it would take away the important meaning of the entire Beatitude. Why would there be a blessing in mourning just so you could quit mourning? I'd prefer not to go through the whole thing.

The word "comforted" is *paraclesis*. Is that a familiar word to you? The Paraclete is the Holy Spirit. *Paraclesis* means "called to one's side." Do you see it beginning to fit together? "Blessed are they that mourn for they shall be called to His side." Now that's exciting! "In thy presence is fullness of joy and at thy right hand (in Jesus) is fullness of joy." I've been called to His side and I'm not leaving. That's a good place to be. "The Lord is nigh unto them that are of a broken heart; and saveth such as be of a contrite spirit" (Ps. 34:18).

"The Lord is nigh unto all them that call upon Him,"—to *all*—and when you read this to someone, make sure you emphasize that word—"to *all* that call upon Him in truth." That's a good verse to memorize.

"That they should seek the Lord, if haply they might feel after him, and find him, though he be not far from every one of us" (Acts 17:27). "Blessed are they that mourn: for they shall be comforted." "Blessed" means "happy, enviable." Why are mourners to be envied? Because "they *shall* be comforted," and this means much more than the person will get over it; it means, "There is a special place for them—right by the side of God himself."

It is the Holy Spirit, the Paraclete, the Comforter who comes not just to soothe your ills, but to take you from a negative experience to the positive side of God. And it is there that we recognize Jesus making true intercession. He's the High Priest and that's our hope. "Blessed are they that mourn: for they shall be comforted."

CHAPTER FOUR

Meekness

BLESSED ARE THE MEEK: FOR THEY
SHALL INHERIT THE EARTH.

(Matt. 5:5)

It's amazing how we overlook the great
truths of the Beatitudes. We put them on
plaques, on bookmarks and carry them with us.
We say, "Those are the Beatitudes," but we
don't really understand their meaning, and the
depth of truth they contain.

"Blessed are the meek: for they shall inherit
the earth." Meekness is very difficult to define.
This is because the word possesses a negative
connotation, and we try to spell it with a W
instead of an M. So we think of a weak person
instead. For example, someone might say,
"There's a very meek man" and what they're
really thinking is, "He doesn't have enough
starch to say what he really thinks." But that is
not the true meaning of meekness.

Vine's *Expository Dictionary of New Testament Words* defines the word "meek" precisely:

> In its use in Scripture, in which it has a fuller, deeper significance than in non-scriptural Greek writings, it consists not in a person's outward behaviour only; nor yet in his relations to his fellow-men; as little in his mere natural disposition. Rather it is an inwrought grace of the soul; and the exercises of it are first and chiefly towards God.

Now that's why we can unequivocally say that meekness is a fruit of the Spirit.

If the Beatitudes are the attitudes we are to be, how do we change from one attitude to another? It is as the Holy Spirit possesses my superego or conscience that I come under divine influence and control. The Bible says that one of the fruits of the Spirit is meekness. Now meekness is an inwrought working of the soul. It isn't just something I do. There are so many illustrations of this. There is the story of the little girl who kept standing up. And the mother said, "Sit down! Sit down!" Finally the mother just reached over and sat her down. And the little girl protested, "I'm standing up inside!" We can understand that, can't we? Have you ever obeyed the Lord and remained "standing up" inside? We all have. That's what meekness is not.

We can all act in certain ways. A common term is being used by some teachers today: "sloppy agape." It is true that we can show all kinds of affection and call it love. We can hug each other's necks and we can smile at one another. We can ask, "How are things going with you?" and never really unmask ourselves. Just like in the cartoon of *The Facade*, we can give to people all in the name of love, never really opening ourselves to them. But that is not what's being spoken of in this Beatitude. Rather, it means when the Holy Spirit comes into our lives, He possesses us. When we ask Him to fill us, we're asking to be possessed by Him!

This truth is expressed in the account of the Annunciation when the angel shared with Mary God's plan for the birth of Christ. Mary's question was, "How shall all of this be?"

The angel explained, "The Holy Spirit shall overshadow thee." That's the cry of my heart and I trust it will become the cry from within each of us. "Overshadow me, Holy Spirit. So they don't see me any more. May they only see the evidence of the Spirit of God who lives within." When He overshadows us, the job gets done!

Since the work of the Holy Spirit is accomplished only when He overshadows us, that's quite a prayer. We certainly need to do some considering before we pray it. In simplistic terms it means: *Jesus Christ is Lord indeed!* A meek individual is one who has appropriated the lordship of Jesus Christ to himself. He no longer rushes to blame the devil for the weather or situations in his life and he doesn't live in constant self-condemnation, saying, "I've done this and I'm wrong, I brought this on myself." But we would be so overshadowed by the Holy Spirit that with reality in spirit and truth he could say, "The Lord has brought this into my life for His purposes."

The Bible tells us that David was meek, but he wasn't always so. Do you remember the time he was encamped with his mighty men when their supplies began to run short (1 Sam. 25)? Since they had been protecting the shepherds and property of Nabal, David thought they could expect some help from that wealthy man. He sent some runners up to tell Nabal what they had been doing and to ask for some food.

Up they went, and approaching Nabal they announced, "Our man David needs some help."

Do you remember Nabal's answer? He

asked, "Who is David?" Now that's what meekness is not!

That's a picture of the world. "Who is God?" "I can do what I want, when I want." "I don't ask God and I don't ask anybody else." "Nabal" means "fool" and this fits him perfectly for he was a very foolish man.

When the word came back to David—at that particular point—he was not totally meek. Read it in Scripture and you will find how extreme his response was. He said, "Put on your swords!" *He was actually ready to kill!* In the meantime, Abigail, Nabal's wife, made her way down to David's camp with meat and fruits. It is a beautiful story of submission and humility. She bowed herself before him and said, "Oh, my lord, please don't pay any attention to my husband and please remember what his name is. Besides, if you go to kill him it will be a blot on your character." Obviously, David was not yet meek.

As time progressed, his own son turned against him, desiring to take the kingdom away from David. Fleeing for their lives, David and his company encountered a man from Saul's family named Shimei who began to curse him and throw stones and dust at him. One of David's mighty men asked, "Who is this dog, that he should be permitted to live? Let me kill him."

But David answered simply, "Let him alone. The Lord has permitted this." Do you see the difference? This is a period of about eighteen years between the two events. David was changing; he was being changed from earthly things to the heavenly—from an uncontrolled spirit to one that was harnessed by the tempering power of God.

The person who has never discovered what it is to be "poor in spirit" has no place to go. That's the first step of the ladder that brings us into the kingdom life. If you think you're rich in spirit and you can do for yourself, there isn't any place for you to go.

A man came to me after a service one evening and said, "That was a very nice little lecture you gave."

I thanked him and then he said, "Oh, well, I'm an atheist."

My answer startled him. "Well, I don't believe in atheists," I said.

He batted his eyes and retorted, "What do you mean, you don't believe in atheists? *I am an atheist!*"

"I don't believe in atheists. I'm sorry. I don't mean to make you angry, but, you see, I don't believe there is such a thing as an atheist."

He was simply ready to kill me. He said, "I'm standing in front of you telling you I'm an atheist!"

I said, "I know how you feel. I'm standing in front of you telling you about Jesus."

After several minutes of conversation, he gave his heart to the Lord! You see, he had this thing called a defense. He had his defenses up in his mind and he needed to be broken in spirit.

A broken spirit reveals to us our sin, and when we are sorry for it—that's the beginning of mourning. Becoming aware that nothing comes into our lives unless it's permitted by the Lord, we step into meekness and this brings release to us. In *How to Be Happy in No Man's Land* I wrote about going into sin and bitterness and meeting a very handsome, six-foot-four, brown-eyed, wavy-haired Marine. I married him, and, in years to come, our home broke up leaving me to raise our two children alone. The Lord, in His mercy and grace, however, brought me back from this place of trouble, taking the negative away and weaving it all into a pattern of beauty for His glory. Those experiences have enabled me to be of help to others. I have some letters on file from people asking, with great hostility, "Are you saying it is God's fault that you were divorced?" No, that's not what I'm saying at all. God knows whatever it will take in our lives to get us from one point to the next, and he will not violate our wills. I can choose not to do right. In the grace of God, no matter what I choose of the negative nature, God says He'll make good out of that.

When I came back to God, I said, "Lord, I don't see how you can use me! I have ruined my whole life. If I can just make it into heaven by the skin of my teeth I would be most grateful." Yet, look at my life today. Isn't it amazing what He can do? This is the understanding of a meek spirit. When in meekness I approach Him and I say, "I don't know what you'll do with me today, and I don't care what you do with me today," then I am released from the obligatory sense that I've got to do something *for* Jesus.

One time I returned to my hotel room and threw myself across the bed in a state of absolute exhaustion and defeat. Every bone and muscle ached. I hurt so deeply and was so weary that I said, "Lord, your Word tells me that your yoke is easy and your burden is light."

A tiny voice inside me declared, *"Mine* is!" I tell you, it was like having a licking; it really was.

So I said, "Well, show me how to walk in *your* yoke." And in my mind's eye I saw the oxen's yoke lift up.

People say, "How do you know when it's the Lord?" I always tell them that anything that is smarter than me has to be from Him. And in my thought process, I heard the Lord say, "I'm the lead ox and all you need to do is put your neck in there."

"Oh, that's wonderful!" I put my neck in, felt that thing clamp down and we started to walk. I didn't have any of the weight. I was just there. I said, "Lord, this is beautiful!"

He replied, "I'm glad you like it. We're turning left at the next corner."

I said, "I'm not."

And, without missing a step, very clearly in my mind He said, "Then you're going to have a broken neck!"

We must become aware that the spirit of meekness says, "Where He goes, I'll go." I have the scars to prove my broken neck. In fact, it's happened so often I don't know if it could be repaired again. But I want to go where He goes, that's all. If Jesus goes with me, I'll go anywhere. And if He doesn't go, I don't want to be there. So the spirit of meekness is totally opposite to pride.

Once a certain rumor was spread about me. It was of such a nature that I could not do one thing about it. To have talked about it would have made it more widespread. This thing went on and it entered a certain circle of influence in which I was scheduled to be involved. I didn't know what to do. I said, "Lord, thy will be done. If you want me to go to these people, just lead me. If you don't, I don't want to go." As the time drew near I wasn't as brave as when I first prayed the prayer but I was still praying it at least through my lips and trying to mean it in my heart. I said, "Lord, now what shall I say to these people?"

The Lord spoke to me: "I want you to ask them to forgive you."

I said, "Lord, if I do that, they'll think I'm guilty. For what am I asking forgiveness?"

He answered me clearly, "You must have done something that showed the very appearance of this thing or it would never have started." I don't know if you can understand how heavy that felt.

Many think prayer is giving God unknown information. I began to tell Him what I thought He didn't know. "Lord, if I do this it won't work." Yet, He said, "That's what I want you to do."

So when I arrived at the meeting, I said, "The Lord has told me to ask you to forgive me."

They looked at me like, "Aha, I knew it was true!"

Then I explained, "I'm seeking your forgiveness because I'm guilty of something that's caused you to accuse me. For that very appearance of evil I ask your forgiveness. Honestly, it isn't because I need *you* so much but it's because I've got to keep the path clear between me and my Lord. I'm in love with Him, and I don't want anything to mar that relationship."

Before we were through in that room the persons who had started this whole thing were on their knees, asking forgiveness. Now that's God! Suppose I had taken *my* way? We would have ended up with factions, each deciding what side to take. What a tragic thing that would have been!

Have you ever been so in need for someone just to love you and instead they just fired one bullet of Scripture after another at you? "So you're depressed. Well, the Bible says—" and using the Word like a machine gun, off they go. Then you're not just depressed—you're half dead also. Thanks a lot.

What does quicken the Word to us? "The Spirit giveth life." This means that when the Spirit of the Lord ministers the Word of the Lord in a spirit of meekness, it involves "speaking the truth in love." "Speaking the truth in love" does not mean, "The only reason I'm telling you this, brother, is that I love you." We can preface any nasty remark with that statement and if it's not true, if we're not meek teachers, it will come across like sounding brass and tinkling cymbals.

That brother will say, "I know she *says* she loves me but somehow what she said just cut me like a knife."

Then we justify that by saying, "Yes, the Word is a two-edged sword."

There is a great challenge in reading the Gospels to see how Jesus dealt with men and women of all backgrounds and educational levels. The only ones with whom He was violent were the hypocrites. He made no bones about it. But they were the religious leaders, who piously stood by in their self-righteous robes pretending to be something they were not.

However, with people who were experiencing failure, problems with their stubborn wills, pride, all of the things that lead people to despair, Jesus came along and said, "Neither do I condemn thee. Now go and sin no more. I love you." He spoke the truth. But He spoke it in love and meekness.

"Seek ye the Lord, all ye meek of the earth, which have wrought his judgment; seek righteousness, seek meekness" (Zeph. 2:3). The Bible tells us to *seek* meekness. When we're told to seek something in the Bible, this indicates that it's not a natural attribute, doesn't it? I don't need to seek something if I have it by nature. The Bible doesn't tell us to seek faith, does it? Instead, the Scripture commands, "Stir it up!" We *have* faith and as we plant faith it grows but it doesn't say that meekness grows; it says, "*Seek* meekness." When we believe that, we begin to pray, "Oh, Lord, let me live with the spirit of meekness flowing from me."

Meekness is so precious in God's sight. In the first book of Peter women are told to not be dependent on external beauty, but on "the hidden man of the heart, in that which is not corruptible, even the ornament of a meek and quiet spirit, which is in the sight of God of great price" (1 Pet. 3:4). Now what does that mean? How often we've heard this misappropriated, misinterpreted, and mistaught. In certain circles, where this has been the teaching, they've pulled it completely out of context, teaching women that they must be totally silent; they shouldn't speak at all in the church; they should speak very little in the home. I don't believe that at all and it's not because I'm a woman. You see, God made us like He did for a purpose. God created women and God created men. God created us in such a way as to be totally complete and yet able to benefit and complement each other. That's why there is marriage.

If a woman is taught that the very assets God has given her are not pleasing to Him, what a tragedy it is. That's one of those diversionary tactics of the enemy.

Women are motivated first by emotion. Men are motivated first by logic. Just study that awhile.

As an example, let's say a vacuum cleaner salesman comes in and he shows us how his product works. The woman's first response is emotional, "Oh, I love it! Let's buy it." The man's initial response, on the other hand, has nothing to do with whether he loves it or not, but he reacts by asking, "Can we afford it?" Then he questions how large the motor is. What kind of guarantee comes with it? How long has the product been on the market?

Men are different from women. That's why I'm so against women's liberation endeavoring to bring sameness into the positions of men and women. We need to understand that this verse in First Peter is talking about meekness as being beautiful in the sight of God. It's expensive. To be God-controlled is expensive. It costs your own will. "I give my will to you, Lord. I'm not my own; I'm yours."

The Lord says, "That's beautiful to me; that's expensive. She gave me a very expensive gift. I'm aware of what that costs, but that's not limited to *women*." That's what God wants from all of His people, men and women alike.

Meekness is necessary if we're going to hear what the Word of God says. Let me read from James: "Wherefore lay apart all filthiness and superfluity of naughtiness, and receive with meekness the engrafted word, which is able to save your souls" (James 1:21).

There's another Scripture which says: "So then because thou art lukewarm, and neither cold nor hot, I will spue thee out of my mouth" (Rev. 3:16).

When I was a young girl, preachers used to dangle us over hell with that verse. "If you're neither hot nor cold, you're going to hell!" It never made sense to me as a youngster. The indication was that if you're cold you don't go to hell and if you're hot you don't go to hell but if you're in between, you've had it! Finally, one day I said, "Lord, what does it mean?" He helped me to become aware of what it meant by watching different congregations.

In the same congregation there can be three people seated right alongside one another. One is hot, which means "turned on to the Spirit of the Lord, fervent in spirit." Another is cold; the individual doesn't even know the Lord. The remaining one has been there and has become indifferent. The person who is hot is excited and thrilled in receiving the Word of God. The individual who is cold often breaks into tears and begins to make preparation to come to know the Lord. But the one who is lukewarm hears nothing. He doesn't understand why you're crying and why you're excited. It's because he's not hearing from the mouth of God.

That may be true of you. You may have

made up your mind to read the Bible, do this and do that, but it's dead and cold to you. If that's true it's because you need to seek *meekness*. You need to come to a position of deciding if you are going to serve Jesus as Lord or not.

I was talking with a young woman and, in essence, she said that's the way things were for her. She couldn't get excited about the things of the Lord, and through counseling, I found out that she was afraid not to serve the Lord but not at all in love with Him. That's being lukewarm. That's tragic. You're the most miserable person on earth when you are in that state.

Did you know that the highest experience we've ever had in God was intended to be our lowest experience from then on? Isn't that incredible? If we'd get a group of people together and ask each to give a testimony about the highest level experience with God they've ever had, we'd hear a variety of experiences. Someone would talk about when he saw an angel. Another person would share about the baptism in the Holy Spirit. Still another would talk about water baptism. But the Father wanted each of these experiences to be stepping stones to a deep relationship with Him rather than the highest experiences of life. When people go back down from a "high" experience, they become unhappy. How do I know? Because people who go back down are seekers. They're seeking, but in the wrong direction. One need only see the problems and promiscuity of our world to realize the truth of this. Most people live graph-like lives—up and down, up and down. Meekness will correct that.

"Lord, I thank you for what I have in you but I honestly pray that I would not be anything like this next year." I really pray that. I don't want to come back to you in a year and be saying the same things to you. I want new things next year. And I can only experience that as I grow in Him.

Be shocked if you will, but I would be able to minister the rest of my life—I really believe—without ever opening the Bible again. I've ministered enough years to know that if I stayed in certain circles I would always be bringing new light to them and I wouldn't have to pray and I wouldn't have to study. But who would be the loser? Of course I would. I want to grow in grace and knowledge.

Now there's a key in that, and meekness will bring us into it. Remember this, to the extent you grow in grace, you will grow in knowledge. That's meekness. Many people want to soar in knowledge and forget grace. Other people want to soar in grace and never *know* anything.

We may have one church on one side of town—they're very harmless—but they don't have any wisdom. We have another church—they're very wise--but they kill you if you don't go their route. The disciples of the Lord were both wise and harmless. That's balance. Growing in grace and knowledge—that's meekness.

The Bible says Moses was the meekest man who ever lived on the face of the earth (Num. 12:3). That's a testimony any of us should love to have. Moses wasn't born meek. Do you remember the first difficulty he had? Moses encountered his first real problem when he saw a Hebrew fighting with an Egyptian, and he stepped out saying, "I'll take over here!" He killed the Egyptian; word went throughout the camp, and suddenly Moses found himself fleeing for his life.

Forty years later he saw something burning. He stepped up to it and the Lord said, "Get your shoes off!" Why? It was holy ground. We have played and toyed around with the things of God long enough. God is going to have a people in every community that please Him. We have churches, churches, churches. We have churches that please this kind of people; we have churches that please that kind of people. In every area, town, city, and county there are churches. But we do not have many churches that please God.

Those who know how to minister unto the Lord (Ezek. 44) and whose first concerns surround God, not community, are few and far between. Not many are going in to the holy place, worshiping and loving Him. Few are found fellowshiping with Him at the table of showbread and then coming out from that relationship and ministering to the people. What's the difference in the two approaches? One priest ministers life to the people because he's been where life is. The other ministers law because that's all he knows.

We have to learn what it is to be in the holy of holies, adoring Him, loving Him, and fellowshiping with Him so that when we come out, people will say, "What's different about your ministry?"

Our answer will be, "All I do is go into His presence. I become absolutely saturated with Him. Then I come out and breathe in and out." That's the call of the Christian—to breathe in and then breathe out.

The earth typifies the land of Canaan. "Blessed are the meek: for they shall inherit the earth." Our first response may be, "Who wants it? Who wants this filthy earth?" But the earth in Scripture is typified by the land of Canaan. When the Lord brought the children of Israel out of Egypt He brought them into Canaan.

While at times we have thought of Canaan as a type of heaven, there never was a promise made to them that Canaan would be free of trouble. There was a consistent battle to possess the wealth of the land and a walk of faith to live in it. In this light Canaan becomes a type of earth. God has not promised us immunity to problems nor the unawareness of them. Yet, there is a position that the believer has which should supersede that of the unbeliever. While living with the awareness that this world is not my home, I'm delighted to realize it is my Father's world. Christians need to learn to enjoy life—seeing its beauty, smelling the flowers, etc. Let creation respond to the Creator.

The land of Canaan has all temporal goods abounding in it. When my desire was for riches and fame and success, I was most unhappy. Twice, during that period of time, I was dispossessed. You know why I had to go through it the second time, don't you? I didn't learn it the first time because I griped all the way. The second time I started to gripe when the Holy Spirit said, "Oh! We're going that route again!" I closed my mouth instantly. I began to praise the Lord through gritted teeth. That's a good beginning. As we begin to give glory to God, the very words reach our ears and we become aware of the truth: "Thou art worthy, O Lord, to receive glory and honour, and power: for thou hast created all things, and for thy pleasure they are and were created" (Rev. 4:11). It wasn't for *our* pleasure. He didn't create everybody on earth to meet *my* needs. He didn't put everything here to bless *me*! He put me here to bless Him! Everything on this earth is to bless Him! That changes our whole attitude toward life!

When I got it all together I really became aware of what that meant. Then I could permit meekness to become a part of my life. I could recognize that I was nothing when I came into the presence of the Lord. Who am I that God should reveal himself to me in a burning bush? Moses was never the same from that moment on and neither were you. Neither was I. From the time I became aware of Him revealing His presence to me—to me, a poor lost sinner who had stubbornly walked away from my childhood training—no, I was never the same again.

We all have problems. Humanity reminds me of the earth when it was without form and void. That's what we are like. "Here I am, Lord. I'm a lump of clay." When I recognize that He is almighty God, when I really recognize this, a spirit of meekness within mandates that I worship Him. We're progressing towards some things in the comprehension of God's Word. I come to God and I say, "I'll live for you who died for me." That's the reciprocal desire which is innate in each of us. Do you remember the day when you became aware that you cannot equalize things with God? The Lord spoke to me and said, "Iverna, do you know the good part of you?"

I responded, "Yes, Lord!"

He answered, "It stinks! It's as filthy rags. Now how do you think they smell? The *good* part of you? The good part? Yes, the good part of you is as filthy rags" (Isa. 64:6).

"Well, then, Lord, I could never have anything from you. I can never be anything." Have you ever gone that little self-pity route in your prayer life? Let me tell you the Scripture to use against that. "Make straight the way of the Lord" (John 1:23). The Old Testament says, "Every valley shall be exalted, and every mountain and hill shall be made low: and the crooked place shall be made straight" (Isa. 40:4). Now I can see the mountains of those people who say, "I sacrificed a lot of things to walk the narrow way, I gave up fame and fortune and I'm worth a lot to thee." That's a mountain—and the Bible says, "Lop it off!"

Have you ever been lopped off? All those exciting things you were going to do for the Lord and suddenly you couldn't do them. The areas of your success failed—that's devastating, isn't it? No, it's leveling.

Then there are the valleys. I think they're worse than the mountains. Because they're the ones that say, "Oh, I could never do anything. I have no talents, no abilities; I can't pray, I can't meet people. I just—you know whatever the Lord wants—but I'm not capable."

And the Lord says, "Fill up that valley! Make straight the way of the Lord."

Now the Bible says, "I can do all things." How? "Through Christ, which strengtheneth me." That is a statement of fact, *period*. As I've shared this truth, I have had people literally break down and bawl.

Do you just want to hold a pity party? Listen, I am proficient in that area. I used to hold them daily for months. I know I am the best pity-party hostess who exists. At our little pity party you tell me all your problems and I say, "Oh, bless your heart, I know what you mean" and I tell you about all my operations and problems. When we get all through, the maximum benefit will be catharsis, which means we got it all out. Would you like once and for all to come out of self-pity?

The Lord says, "Iverna, give me your ashes and I'll give you beauty."

"Lord, give me the beauty and I'll give you the ashes."

He replies, "No, you give me the ashes first."

I say, "Lord, if I gave you my ashes, what

would I talk about? What would I pray?"

You know, we spend the first moment of prayer going through our ashes. We say, "Lord, I've never done this, but I'm sorry for having done that and I know you've forgiven me but," and then we go through our ashes.

The Lord says, "If you ever get sick of your ashes, I'll give you beauty for them. If you'll give up that spirit of heaviness, I'll put a garment of praise on you" (Isa. 61:3).

There's a song we used to sing in my church. One of the verses says, "Though the way seems straight and narrow, All I claimed was swept away; My ambitions, plans, and wishes at my feet in ashes lay." The very next line of that song is: "I will praise Him! I will praise Him! Praise the Lamb for sinners slain!"

"Now, what's wrong with that songwriter?" you may ask. "Doesn't she understand?" Yes, she does understand. She's given up ashes and received beauty and there's no problem with a songwriter saying, "To God be the glory, great things He hath done."

Moses, from the time he encountered God, only had to hear the voice of God to say, "God hath done this, God hath done that, God hath done the other thing." That's what the spirit of meekness will say.

What are the rewards of meekness?

The meek shall eat and be satisfied:
they shall praise the Lord that seek
him: your heart shall live for ever. (Ps.
22:26)

It's exciting to eat and be satisfied.
Spiritually, we begin to understand this. We
begin to realize that there are people who are
eating and they're not being satisfied at all.

The Lord lifteth up the meek. (Ps.
147:6)

That's an amazing thing! The Lord has been
trying to promote us and satisfy us by giving us
the earth, all of the provisions of life. We can't
handle it, because the minute He gives us an
army we brag on it. The minute He gives us a
provision we brag on it. "Gideon, you've got too
many! Thirty thousand—that's too many
people. If you win the war with them, *you'll* take
all the credit. How about three hundred?"
(Judges 7)

Strip. Strip. Strip. I say, "Lord, I have
nothing left!"

He says, "Good, now you'll know everything
you have is from me." That's meekness. When
the Lord brings us down, or permits us to bring
ourselves down—the moment meekness
becomes a part of our living—He begins to lift
us up and He promotes whom He will (Ps.
75:6-7).

Many people have learned how to be abased, but they have never learned how to abound. Paul said, "I know both how to be abased, and I know how to abound" (Phil. 4:12). When you have meekness in your life, it doesn't matter. One minute you're rich; the next minute you're not rich. It simply doesn't matter.

> But with righteousness shall he judge the poor, and reprove with equity [which means fairness] for the meek of the earth. (Isa. 11:4)

This means we're getting a fair deal with God. That's hard to believe. I've not always seen that in the Word. In fact, there was a day when I heard a man preach that when you're under the dealings of God, you should never expect a fair shake. I believed that, and I was going through some things then. It may be true *immediately* but not *ultimately*. While we're going through it it does not seem fair. But the reason it's fair is because God, who is doing it, is going to bring so much beauty out of it. He's going to be able to give us the very desires of our hearts, because He has instilled within us a quality we didn't possess before and He's going to be able to bring it to good for His glory.

The meek also shall increase their joy

in the Lord. (Isa. 29:19)

I'm ready to seek meekness, aren't you? I want to be God-controlled. I want God to rule and reign over every thought and intent of my heart and over every action of my life. When we come to that understanding, we're ready to counsel, we're ready to teach, we're ready to flow. When we know that kind of victory in our lives, we're ready to share it with others. Now we can understand a higher meaning to the "meek shall inherit the earth."

There has been much teaching recently on the kingdom of God and while it is my personal belief that man cannot establish God's kingdom, I do believe we can recognize it.

In recognizing it we become aware of what Jesus meant when He said, "Other sheep I have, which are not of this fold: them also I must bring . . ." (John 10:16) and the promise of Psalm 2:8, "Ask of me, and I shall give thee the heathen for thine inheritance, and the uttermost parts of the earth for thy possession."

The entire thrust of our missionary concern must be based on this inheritance.

Let us remember that this promise of inheritance is to the meek rather than to the qualified. Are we mature enough to become aware of that instead of "winning souls" we are claiming our inheritance?

CHAPTER FIVE

A Hungering and Thirsting Spirit

BLESSED ARE THEY WHICH DO
HUNGER AND THIRST AFTER
RIGHTEOUSNESS: FOR THEY SHALL
BE FILLED. (Matt. 5:6)

In Matthew 5:1 we see that Jesus called the people and healed them before He began teaching them. This is a consistent principle in His involvement in our lives.

First, He calls us unto himself and then He begins to heal us. He starts the healing in our sin-sick souls by taking care of our sins. Then He works on our inhibitions, scars, defeats, etc.; that's what is being termed "inner healing" today. The title might be new, but inner healing itself isn't new. The Lord's been healing in this manner from the beginning of time. He commences from within, taking the negatives from our lives and allowing us to see the beauty of brokenness they have produced. Once held in the Master's hand, the brokenness is prepared for His remolding. Our Master potter never leaves a vessel empty. At this point we are prepared to receive His instructions.

We can't start backwards. First, we're called and then we're healed and after that we're taught. It's not a "once and for all" situation. Those are three steps we repeat all through our lives. From level to level to level. From faith to faith to faith. From glory to glory to glory. From plateau to plateau to plateau.

The Beatitudes are the divine influence and divine nature imparted to God's people. How does the Lord bring His nature into my nature? By experience—through the Holy Spirit. It can come from somebody talking to us on the phone or in person. Once in a meeting when I shared about being dispossessed, there was a brother who told me that he had been cheated in business. He had lost absolutely everything and in the process he made the decision to sue. He had already seen attorneys and was going to sue for half a million dollars and he had a pretty good chance of getting it. As he was making his final contact with the attorney, the Lord said, "No, don't sue for it." Of course, when we hear from God in a matter such as this we feel that God's going to give it back to us. But the end of that particular case was that the businessman was stripped bare. He said it was because he had a richness in his spirit.

We can never give a blanket promise to people. We did in the early days of Pentecost—we used to say to people, "If you accept Jesus as your personal Savior, He'll heal your marriage or your finances." We were sincere, but we did not tell the truth. People would get up by the dozens, coming forward to accept the Lord as their personal Savior. Then they'd go back out, find their marriages still broken up, their finances still not together and they would turn away from God. They said, "We were promised something we didn't get!" Jesus never guaranteed immunity from problems for the Christian. Never, but He did pledge, "I will never leave you alone. I'll go with you and I will bring peace to your life if you'll appropriate it."

Usually, when we are able to handle things again, He will give them back to us. But when my husband divorced me and married another woman I no longer held hope for the marriage. I hear women doing this—"Oh, someday he'll divorce her and marry me again!" The Bible doesn't teach that two wrongs make a right. There are some things we just have to let go as a part of life, part of the pattern, part of sin, part of our past. There are always scars connected with sin.

Some people say, "You cannot come to this

place in the Lord unless you have been broken." But, you see, it takes different things to break different people. I raised a daughter, all I had to do and all I still have to do (even though she's married) is just look at her a certain way and she's broken. She's extremely tender by nature. She does not want to displease her mother or anyone else on earth. My son has to be hit with a two-by-four before he responds. We're the same way with the Lord. Some people recognize their need as soon as conviction hits them. They weep before God and they come the easy route. The rest of us. . . .

We have to bring people back to an awareness of who God is. God is God almighty. We don't boss Him around. Then why do some people get by with doing it? For the same reason that an infant in our home gets by with it. When the President of the United States has a child and the baby cries, the president runs in to meet the baby's needs. But that doesn't last when the tiny child gets older. There are other schoolmasters, other tutors, other nurses in charge. We have to learn to obey others. So when an adult, who has already met and known the Lord, is bawling because he told God to do something and He didn't do it, the person needs to see God as being almighty.

Isn't it time for us to say, "He is Lord"? We

can bring our wants and our wishes and our needs to Him. But we must be willing to receive from Him what He gives. You see, He's not our butler; He's our God. Prayer doesn't ring a bell and put Him at our beck and call. Prayer is communion with Him. "Lord, I love you; oh, how I love Jesus." In effect, that's prayer and praise and we need to teach people this. Otherwise we may as well talk about Santa Claus; that would be easier. The big, good-natured, jolly man in the sky. That's the idea many people have of God. And it's not a true idea and it's not the revelation God gave. The very names of God define who He is. "I am that I am."

When my son was four we lived in an apartment. I said to him, "What would you like for Christmas?"

Immediately he answered, "I'd like a pony." It didn't make sense, did it?

When he was fourteen, I said, "What would you like for Christmas?"

He answered, "What could we afford?" A sense of maturity had come into his life.

We must come to a level of maturity where we know what we're asking for from the Lord, instead of: "I want Christmas today!" Some of us live that way with Him. But promises are made to *sons*. When we begin to become aware of that we can help others see it. That's why I say, "It's too bad we have supposedly mature Christians who are running from miracle-worker to miracle-worker while saying, "I'm growing up in the Lord!" No, you're not; you're playing kindergarten, having a good time and saying, "Whee! Look at the magic!"

Now it's an impressive and thrilling reality to see God do what seems impossible. That's a miracle and it's exciting. But we can't live on excitement.

Some of you have raised children and you know that when they reach their teens, they are up one day and down the next. In fact, they're up one hour and down the next. And the reason is that they want life. Their whole bodies and physical systems are excited during those difficult years and they want to be constantly stimulated. "Let's get something going; let's get the action on!"

I observe the same thing in the church of the Lord Jesus Christ. I see a bunch of teen-agers trying to be adults. "Let's get it going! Let's get the pastor out and get another one in. We need an evangelist!" What we need to do is stand still long enough to be rooted so we don't appear as trees that are moving. Remember when Jesus first touched a blind man, asking him what he saw?

His answer was, "I see men as trees walking" (Mark 8:24).

The Bible says, "He shall be like a tree planted by the rivers of water" (Ps. 1:3). That's what God's trying to do with us—plant us. That's what we've got to do with others, because I believe time has been shortened. We have the same amount of hours in a day that we had twenty years ago. We have modern conveniences to do what we did manually twenty years ago, but we don't get half as much done today. Rushing, rushing, but what did you get done today? Time has been shortened, and because of this we have an increased responsibility to others. We've got to get people into the Word of God and help them to recognize that the living waters are a type of the Word and the Spirit. Water, in the Bible, is always a type of the Word and a type of the Spirit. We need to get people planted, grounded, and founded by these living waters.

In Matthew 4 Jesus called His disciples and the Bible tells us He healed the multitudes. I'm suggesting the principle that first He calls us, then He heals us, then He teaches us. That will be a continuous process of life. In all of our maturity in the Lord, we will find first the call. How does He call us? By the Holy Spirit. Why do we know the Holy Spirit is calling us? Because we have the desire to be called.

Jesus said, "Blessed—in an enviable position—are you if you *desire me*, if you hunger and thirst after my whole nature." It is by His righteousness that we come. Have you ever met anyone who wanted to desire Him but didn't? I have. People have come to me and said, "Sister, I would give anything if I could have what you declare you possess—a hunger after God. I don't have it."

I say to them, "You're on the first step. You're putting aside your own spirit. You're becoming poor in spirit and you're getting ready now to say, 'Lord, I want to want.'" That's a valid prayer. "I want to want you." As you begin to pray for a hungering and thirsting spirit, you become aware that you can't even want Him without His enablement with which to want. You can't love Him without His love. You need to ask Him: "Would you give me your love so I can love you?"

What does His word say about that? It says, "Herein is love, not that we loved God but that he loved us, and sent his Son to be the propitiation for our sins" (1 John 4:10).

And I say, "Oh, that's right; Lord, would you give it to me because I think I love you and I'd like to give it back." And where He imparts His love to me, it's just like a constant flow through me. I love Him, for He is mine.

The Song of Solomon says: "Draw me, and I will run after thee!" We become delighted with the hungering and thirsting spirit. A lady came to me in Hawaii when I was there ministering and she told me this story: "When I was a young woman I used to weep. I enrolled in a Bible school and I used to cry between classes. I didn't know what was wrong with me. I went to my professors and I asked them to help me. Nobody seemed to understand my problem. I never felt satisfied. I wept all the time. Because I couldn't get any help, I said, 'Lord, I'm tired of crying. I don't want to weep any more.' My tears dried up like a waterless well."

She went on to say, "Sister, that was ten years ago. I would give anything I own if I could shed a tear." I looked at her and compassion began to rise from within me. As I was weeping, I stood and looked at her because I could identify with her. I said, "I believe God is going to break this wall you've built around yourself and I believe you're going to cry again. But I'm going to tell you something. If He ever gives you back a hungering and thirsting spirit that causes you to respond towards Him in softness and desire, I want you to use it only to seek Him with."

She said, "I will!" I took her hands and prayed a short prayer and then I was hurried off to another meeting. Within two weeks a letter came from her in which she wrote, "The tears are flowing and the joy is being reaped, and I bless my Lord that I am once again hungering and thirsting after Him!"

As I travel all over the United States, people constantly come to me and say, "I'm so tired of being hungry."

I say, "Wait a minute! Be very careful what you're saying. You're not tired of being hungry. You just want to be satisfied." Someone has put it this way: "I am satisfied with an unsatisfactory satisfaction." That's the way I like it! I feel satisfied with Jesus but I'm not satisfied with my satisfaction. I want more and more of Jesus.

That's how it works; less of me and more of Him. Why? Payback? No. Reciprocation? Negative. When I take *me* out there's more room for Him. Did you ever sing, "Fill My Cup, Lord" and hold up just a thimble? Some of us seem to have no capacity for God! We're all filled up with life and problems and programs and ideologies and philosophies and all the other things. We need to say, "I want *you*, Lord."

He says, "I'm in the only area you have opened to me." So that's when the bulldozer comes. "Dig me deep and dig me wide 'cause I want to be a channel for the river of God."

You say, "I don't understand. You see, I've never been as close to God as I am now and then my marriage broke up." Or "I've never been as close to God as I am now and I've just gone broke" or "I've become ill in my body"—or whatever. That can be frustrating to Christians. You felt filled with God but didn't realize that it's His intention to increase your capacity for himself.

Ecclesiastes 3:3 tells us there's a time to break down and a time to build up. What a delight it is to know that the times are in His hand. We cannot decide to control our own lives without becoming submerged in introspection which produces only self-condemnation. When we yield to His working in our lives, we can rest beside Him in the boat as the storm rages about us, knowing that He will perfect that which concerns us (Ps. 138:8).

The Bible speaks of vessels. There are vessels of wrath and vessels of honor. There are vessels of dishonor also. The vessel of honor was a five-gallon container that sat in the homes of all the people in the Middle East. This vessel was to be picked up every day and carried to the springs, filled with fresh water and brought back for the family's use. It was standard procedure that if you saw anyone bearing a vessel of honor and they were on their way from the spring, you could stop them and say, "May I have a drink of water?"

Now the Bible says *we're* vessels of honor. And so that means that we should walk about being filled with fresh spring water all the time, so that at any moment anyone who needs a drink can ask us to pour for them. Isn't that exciting? However, there is one consideration. The shape of the vessel was rounded on the bottom, so in order for someone to find it useful he had to reach down and grasp it with both hands, support it and get it to his lips. He had to support it to pour out from it for washing and so on. After many days and weeks of use the potter upon entering the house would spot the vessel of honor and say, "Aha, I need to take that back to the shop."

At it's most useful period of time the vessel would be emptied out, taken to the potter's shop, where the first tool he used on it was the file. The potter would file away all the dirt that had come from many hands, and smooth the rough edges. Then, when he finished all the filing, he would sand it until no ridges could be seen where they had once marred the vessel.

Have you ever been filed? Scrape, scrape, scrape, scrape. The Lord puts us through the same process, and when we're all clean again He puts us back in the furnace for one more firing.

Can you identify with that? It should help you—it did me when I discovered a book that explained it. I began to understand why it is that when I'm at my highest peak of usefulness to Him and flowing in God—not in stubborn rebellion but in His will—suddenly: Bam! Put back on the shelf! I say, "I can't live through this, God. I won't live, God. I tell you, I'll break!" He just keeps filing until He's all through and I think I'm going back to usefulness, then I find myself in the furnace again. I say, "God, if you turn this heat up, I'll melt!"

He replies, "I hope so!"

And that also is not a one-time operation. We're not super-spiritual beings. Just plain humans, who possess the Spirit of God. We do pick up man's ways. And we are pressured by people and churches and programs and all of these things. They do leave their marks on us. And the Lord says, "That's all right. I know exactly how to clean you up."

Now the only way we can appreciate such a program is to have such a hunger and such a thirst for God that nothing short of himself satisfies us.

This word "hunger" means pinching toil. Another source describes it as being excruciating—something that makes you feel like you're going to die if you don't get released from it. It's a very strong word.

"Blessed are they who have this kind of hunger," the Word says. Then there's thirst. And here's what one man said about it: "It means the ardent, eager, famishing, keen and all-consuming craving and passion of the soul for complete union with God and fulness of the

Spirit." That's a heavy, isn't it?

When we come to that position, we fall on our faces before God and say, "I'm not getting up from this place until I find God." When we do that, we *will* find God. As we go to that same spot and say, "I'm not getting up from this place until I get an answer," we may stay a long time.

Some people go on hunger strikes and call it fasting. What's the difference? A hunger strike says, "This is what I want and I'm not eating till I get it!" And they call it a fast.

A true fast says, "Lord, I'm going to deprive this flesh, this self; I'm going to bring myself into subjection that I may prove to me that I can rule over myself and I'm longing for you." Do you see the difference?

There's so much emphasis on fasting today. People are being taught that they can twist God's arm by not eating. The Bible says, "That's not the kind of fast I'm looking for. I'm looking for souls to worship me, to bring sacrifices of praise and offerings that way to me." This ardent thirst after God is described in the Word of God in so many ways: "As the hart panteth after the water brooks, so panteth my soul after thee, O God" (Ps. 42:1). Another one is: "Oh God, thou art my God; early will I seek thee: my soul thirsteth for thee, my flesh longeth for thee in a dry and thirsty land, where no water is" (Ps. 63:1).

It's important for us to recognize that God entrusts us sufficiently to pluck us out of a place where there is milk and honey flowing—where the blessing of the Lord is, where teaching and preaching and ministry and praise and worship are flowing. When God puts us there—that's Elim. That's our time. If you're in Elim, drink up because it won't last forever. Have a good time. Slurp it up; eat all you can. Bathe in the sun, because one day before you realize it, He's going to pluck you from that thing. And then you're going to be in a dry, thirsty land. You'll be looking around and thinking, "Where's the well in this place? Don't you have a church that flows?"

"I don't know. What's a church that flows?"

And you begin to question. "Where's the nearest place where they pray?"

The Lord says, "Under your feet."

"You mean, dig a well?"

"Abraham did."

And we begin to say, "My soul thirsteth for God in a dry and thirsty land."

He says, "Then keep digging. You're going to hit water one of these days."

Listen, there aren't many well-diggers left, but thank God there are a few. I thank God He has men and women everywhere, all over this world, who are willing to begin to dig with whatever tool God gives them. To dig until they begin to see the living waters trickle from beneath them. And they recognize that their spiritual hunger drove them to do something about it, instead of looking for a church that could be a hospital for them.

Do you realize that most of us were brought up in intensive-care units? We were force-fed, whether we wanted to eat it or not. The Word was made so palatable it was taken out of the shell and ground up, then they pried our mouths open with the songs and crammed it in and pushed it clear down into us so we wouldn't choke. Intensive care, wasn't it?

Jesus said, "They that be whole need not a physician." Just those who are sick. And then He said to the leaders, "But go and learn what this means. Go find out what I'm saying."

I'm beginning to see that He's coming for a church without spot or wrinkle. He's coming for a mature bride. He's not coming for children. He's coming for a bride and He's trying to help us grow up so He will be able to adorn us with bridal ornaments. Then He will come back and say, "Now you're ready to belong to me throughout all eternity."

We have to learn how to dig when we're thirsty. We don't stand out here and say, "Oh, my soul thirsteth for God in a dry and thirsty land. Oh, come and dig a well." He says *you do it*.

How do you dig a well? By using the Word of God, the faith that is within you and praise. The way you live and the way you speak become praise to His glory. And with praise and prayer and supplication and thanksgiving you have balance. They are the oars in the boat of faith. What way do people go who use just one oar? In circles. So we've got one church—they really praise, but they don't pray—they're not going anywhere. Then we have another church and they don't praise but they sure do pray. And they're going around the other way. And God says, "My church will get in my boat of faith and with the oars of prayer and praise begin to pull toward my destiny for them. They shall come to maturity."

The same principle is true in digging a well. We appropriate prayer and praise and the Word of God. We stand upon the Word of God. "God, it's not what I say, but what you say." When we begin to pray with that kind of determination, the voice of Jesus comes to us and says, "Blessed are ye who hunger and thirst for you're in an enviable state. Not everybody has that kind of determination, but *you* have it; you're very fortunate indeed."

Peter spoke to babies. He said, "As newborn babes, thirst after milk." But when you go beyond babyhood—isn't it sad when you see a person who only wants to live on milk? We need

THE WAY TO HAPPINESS

to learn to eat the meat of the Word.

You may not understand all that I'm talking about. Good, I hope you get thirsty and hungry and begin to dig it out so that you can understand it because there is so much more than what I'm able to share with you that God wants to share with you. "Behold, the days come, saith the Lord God, that I will send a famine in the land, not a famine of bread, nor a thirst for water, but of hearing the words of the Lord" (Amos 8:11).

"A famine for the hearing of the Word of the Lord? Iverna, that can't be today. Are you kidding? We've got more books, more tapes, more traveling ministers, more teachers, more preachers, more evangelists, more miracles than we've ever had in our lives." Wait a minute! It does not say a famine *of* the Word of God. It says a famine of the *hearing* of the Word of God.

Well, church, there is a vast difference between the Word of God being spoken and the Word of God being heard. May God anoint the ears of His own people to hear. Listen, it's not hard for God to get people saved. It's not difficult. It is done in heaven. It's sealed. Calvary and the resurrection paid the price! It's all paid for! There are people who have their names written in God's book who haven't even claimed it yet. Do you believe that? Then one day they're going to wake up and say, "Oh,

God, be merciful to me, a sinner." And the gift of salvation is given. Do you know why we don't have them coming by the thousands right now? Because He doesn't have many parents in the body of Christ. We're still sitting around sucking our little thumbs and our pacifiers and pouting every time we don't get our own way. Withdrawing our tithes from the church when they say the wrong thing and switching churches because they didn't go the way we voted. That's babyhood. You cannot give birth to an infant and put the infant in the lap of a baby and expect anything but malnutrition.

And so the Word of the Lord is being spoken to the church today. Some are getting saved but nothing like what we're going to see. I believe in our lifetime there's going to be one of the greatest influxes in history of people meeting Jesus as their personal Savior.

When I first started traveling and ministering, ministers and people used to come to me and say, "You know, you've got a good word but really you should be emphasizing salvation and the infilling of the Holy Spirit. You seem to always minister just to the believer."

I thought, "Maybe they're right." Then I remembered sitting in a church for years, being treated as if I hadn't any maturity at all. Every message that came was, "Get to know

Jesus as your personal Savior." So I used to get saved every week. What else was there to do? So I said, "Lord, what's the answer to this?"

He said, "I'm trying to get parents ready. I'll bring forth the birth; that's not hard for me to do. I'll bring babies into your churches. Your church will grow; your prayer groups will grow."

We must have that hungering, thirsting spirit that is called a "passion, an inner passion." So we might long for God. How do we long for God? Well, it depends. If we're on a junior level, we long for God to give to us. If we're at an intermediate level we long for God to let us. "Please, can't I go here? Please, can't I go there? Please, can't I have that?" Do you see the difference? One is looking for gifts. The other is looking for permission to do what he wants to do. But when we come into maturity, and we say, "My soul thirsteth for God," we just want to be with Him. That's what we're saying, "God, I just want to be with you."

Have you ever been away from home over a period of time and then called back to your loved ones? I remember calling my son when I was on the road. I said, "I am so lonesome for you."

"Why?" he asked.

I said, "Don't say that. It makes me think you're not lonesome for me."

"Of course, I'm lonesome for you," he assured me, "but why are you lonesome for me?"

"I don't know," I answered. "I just want to be with you."

Did you ever feel that way about a loved one? I didn't particularly want to *say* anything to him; I just wanted to sit beside him or have his big, tall body stand beside me and have him hit me on the back of the head like he does and say, "You know, you're not all that bad!" That's a compliment! I miss that when I'm on the road. I get lonely for him.

That's what happens when we grow up in the Lord. And when I don't spend time every day in fellowship with Jesus, I just get lonesome. I used to be frustrated in my prayer life, because I didn't have a need to present to Him. How could I come to Him if I didn't have a need? Make one up? Have you ever done it? You don't have to make up a need to come to Jesus. You simply come and say, "Hi. Oh, I love you. I love you so much!" It's so good to wake up and know He's there. It's so good to go to sleep and know He's there. It's so good to walk with Him and fellowship with Him and talk with Him and commune with Him and I can't stand it when He hides himself even for one hour, because my soul thirsts for God.

Jesus dealt with every person He

encountered from their vantage point, not from His. He went to the Pharisees and laid them out. Why? Because they were religious leaders. When you are a leader there is a greater responsibility. The Lord dealt with them right from their realms of hypocrisy. "You really know the Scriptures, do you boys? Searching the Scriptures for in them ye think ye have life." Wow! But He didn't talk that way to the little adulteress, did He? He said, "Woman, what seems to be the problem here?"

"Well, sir, I was taken in adultery." Then He gave a little time for her accusers to wait for His great club to fall in the same manner that they had heard Him speak to the Pharisees. But He just messed around in the sand a little bit and then said, "All right, here's my vote. Let him without sin among you cast the first stone." The crowd dispersed. "Woman, where are thine accusers?"

"Sir, you're the only one left."

"Neither do I condemn thee. Go, and let's end it right here."

Then there was the woman at the well. He began to talk to her. "Give me a drink."

"A Jew would talk to me, a Samaritan woman?"

"If you knew who you were talking to you would have asked me for a drink." Jesus proceeded to talk to her about living water.

What was He doing? He was calling her. He was creating a thirst in her, wasn't He?

Have you ever been with some friend when you are on a diet, and they say, "How would you like to have a nice, gooey hot fudge sundae?" What are they doing? They're creating a hunger for something. In Jesus' case, He was creating a hunger for something she *could* have. She didn't believe she could have it for she was a Samaritan, and not too well received in her social field either. And Jesus began to deal with her and finally He said to her, "Go get your husband."

She replied, "Sir, I don't have a husband."

He said, "You're not kidding. You've had five and the one you're living with, you didn't even bother to legalize." Now that's a pretty extreme case, isn't it? So, if you think *you* can't make it, remember this woman. Five and a half husbands and yet Jesus said, "Let's talk about worship. My father is Spirit; they that worship Him must worship in spirit and in truth." Why? Because the woman had a craving and she didn't know what to do with that craving so she looked in the bedroom for what she could only find in the prayer room.

Whatever way we choose to go, God's Word assures us that He will set about to instruct us in that way. That's a good promise. "Lord, I want to know you."

He always answers, "I hear that prayer." He then begins to put teachers and pastors and tapes and books and situations—whatever is necessary—in our path to show us His ways. "What man is he that feareth the Lord? Him shall the Lord teach in the way that he should go" (Ps. 25:12). Or another way of saying it is, "Blessed are they who hunger and thirst after righteousness, for they shall be filled."

CHAPTER SIX

Being Merciful

BLESSED ARE THE MERCIFUL: FOR
THEY SHALL OBTAIN MERCY. (Matt.
5:7)

I begin every day with a prayer something
like this: "Lord, let me please you today
in everything I say, in everything I do, in
everything I feel. Let me please you." And that
is the only way I have of trusting me. If I didn't
check that motivation before I left my room
and you encountered me and said, "Why are
you going there today?" I might begin to doubt
myself.

Begin your day by checking your motivations
for that day. What is it that you want to
accomplish and why? Are you in love with
Him? If so, you will want to please Him.

We need to develop the habit pattern of
asking for God's help before each task. Being
on television frightens me. I'm scared to death

when I know I'm going to be on the air. I do everything I can to not be there. Before one appearance, nobody came after me so I felt released from the responsibility of going until they called. I sat there waiting, not knowing when, how, or what it would be. I prayed in tongues for guidance and peace and the flowing of His life through me. Now if you were watching me you could not see that, but behind my smile it was a different story. We need to learn to do this—to pray for wisdom and anointing because the last thing we want to do is to go out and do less than our Master wants us to do. Maybe it will work for you to develop that little habit pattern of praying, "Lord, speak your Word through me today."

"Blessed are the merciful for they shall obtain mercy." *Eleeo* is the Greek word for mercy and it means "to feel sympathy with the misery of another." It is especially a kind of sympathy that is manifested in action. It's one thing to sympathize and another thing to do something with it. In Latin it's *miseracordia*—pitying and heart. So it's a heart that pities but not in the negative, condescending way we often use the word "pity." Not negatively, but "as the Lord pitieth his children." With the tender compassion, the deep care, the special concern, the genuine feeling toward you by God. From deep within, caring so much and willing to do something about it.

Mercy is an attribute of God. You'll find that in several Scriptures:

> But the mercy of the Lord is from everlasting to everlasting upon them that fear him. (Ps. 103:17)

> For thy mercy is great above the heavens. (Ps 108:4)

> Not by works of righteousness which we have done but according to his mercy he saved us. (Titus 3:5)

Mercy is God's very nature. When we say it's an attribute of God, we're actually saying it's a part of Him. It's that part of God which puts genuine concern into action, and it's exciting. The same Greek word is translated "compassion" in Matthew 18:33, Mark 5:19 and Jude 22.

Mercy comes from God. It is a part of God. It is God in us, and it's a very beautiful thing. Mercy is attitude plus action. It's forgiveness with the right attitude. True forgiveness. It differs from a forgiveness that suggests we can forgive a person and not do anything for them. We just forgive them and that's that. They may never know we've forgiven them. But we can handle that and get ourselves set free, even though we may keep them in bondage. True mercy is not that way. It's not limited to *me*. Mercy comes forth from me to another individual.

There is a story of a king and a servant in which a servant owed a king considerable money. Coming to the king he said, "Oh, sir, please have patience with me and I will pay thee all."

The king answered, "All right, I'm going to have mercy on you. I forgive it."

So the servant went out rejoicing that his debt was paid in full (Matt. 18:23-35). Do you understand how that relates to us? I owed a debt I could not pay. Jesus paid a debt He did not owe. So I come out absolutely free from the responsibility of all my sin. I've been set free by the grace of God and the blood of Jesus and I can clap and sing.

But then the time comes when somebody owes me money, somebody hurts me, somebody owes me something, and I'll forgive them when they come and ask. That's not mercy.

Continuing with our account of the king's servant, we discover a man in debt to him for the smallest fraction of the amount. Now this man says to the servant, "Please, sir, have

patience with me, and I will pay thee all." But
the king's servant would not and had him
thrown in prison.

When the king heard about it, he said, "Then
withdraw from him the mercy I showed him,
and throw him in prison. Let the jailers
torment him until he pays all." Why? We have it
right before us. "Blessed are the merciful, for
they shall obtain mercy." I can't live without it.
Every day He mixes up a new batch.

"Thy compassions fail not, and thy mercies
are renewed every day" (Lam. 3:22-23). I use
mine up every day—the mercy that has to be
poured out upon us. But if I will not be
merciful, I cannot receive mercy.

Recall with me the account of that man of
God, Stephen, in Acts 7:54-60. "When they
heard these things, they were cut to the heart
and they gnashed on him with their teeth"
(Acts 7:54). That's most extreme, isn't it? I've
never had anyone gnash at me. They were so
pricked, so convicted, so upset with what
Stephen was saying that they literally gnashed
on him with their teeth. Suppose today—you're
doing what God told you to do, sharing what
God told you to share. Everything is right,
you're minding God and you're saying, "He
will protect me. The Lord will take care of me.
No matter where I go, the Lord will take care of
me." Suddenly your listeners pounce upon you

unto death. What do you do? Do you get mad at God? Or do you get mad at the people? Or do you begin to check your life and see if there is sin in it. Maybe you really hadn't done what God said after all. You probably really weren't called in the first place. Do you ever have that thought?

"He, being full of the Holy Ghost, looked up stedfastly into heaven, and saw the glory of God, and Jesus standing on the right hand of God, And said, 'Behold, I see the heavens opened, and the Son of man standing on the right hand of God.' Then they cried out with a loud voice, and stopped their ears, and ran upon him with one accord, And cast him out of the city, and stoned him: and the witnesses laid down their clothes at a young man's feet, whose name was Saul" (Acts 7:55-58).

Anyone who rejects light hates it; anyone who rejects illumination, revelation, light detests them. On the contrary, anyone who embraces or longs for light is excited with it. But if I don't want to see it, I reject it and the source from whence it came. If you're the one that showed it to me, I hate you, unless I'm going to embrace the light.

Are you prepared for that? Are you prepared for people to hate you because you have illuminated them? If not, get ready. *It really is going to happen*. And this will be true more and more, because darkness is waxing greater and greater. Filthiness is becoming filthier and filthier. "He that is unjust, let him be unjust still: and he which is filthy, let him be filthy still" (Rev. 22:11). It is happening.

But by the same token, holiness is getting holier. We're becoming aware that holiness doesn't consist in how we dress and where we go and what we don't do. Holiness is again the very attribute of God. Christ in me is illumination. And Christ was in Stephen revealing light. The people did not want that light. And so they gnashed on him. They stoned Stephen. Stephen was calling upon God and saying, "Lord Jesus, receive my spirit." What's wrong with this man? Isn't he bright? What a prayer; why is he praying that? Because he's in the kingdom. He's already become aware of the fact that everything that happens to him is going to bring God glory. He had checked his motivation that morning when he got up. He had said, "Let my life or my death bring glory to your name, Lord Jesus." He's not mad at the people; he doesn't even think about that.

"And he kneeled down and cried with a loud voice, Lord, lay not this sin to their charge" (Acts 7:60). That is mercy. How can a man do this? Easy. There are seven steps:

1. Be full of the Holy Ghost. We need this to

be a consistent daily filling, not just a one-time experience of being baptized in the Holy Spirit. The verb tense in Ephesians 5:18 insists that we keep on being filled.

2. Look steadfastly up. Keep God as your focal point. Keep Jesus in your eye. The light of the body is the eye. What we look at is what we become full of. If we look at the people—"They're going to kill me, Lord"—we've had it. But just look steadfastly up. The Lord is our defense. The Lord is our high tower. "The Lord is my light and my salvation, of whom shall I be afraid?" (Ps. 27:1)

3. See God's glory—that's the presence of God. The *shekinah* was the evidence of the presence of God. We need to learn to practice the presence of God.

4. See Jesus as He is, not as you picture Him. You'll grow in the revelation of this. Many people see Him as different artists have painted Him. Some of you see Him as the big policeman in the sky, others as a healer, etc. Your concept of God will limit your relationship to Him. Is he a Savior? The answer is yes. But is He a Savior only? The answer is no. Is He Savior, healer, baptizer? Yes, of course. But is that all you know about Him? Then you don't know Him well. Begin to see the heavens open. See Him crowned King of kings and Lord of all. And if you've lost sight of the vision

reread Revelation 1.

5.   Declare your faith. "I see Jesus; I feel the stones, I feel the gnashing, but I see Jesus. I see Him high and lifted up, and His train fills the temple." Let's *see Jesus,* and speak what we know to be true.

6.   Commend your spirit to God. In life or in death. "Blessed are the poor in spirit." How do you get poor in spirit? Give it to God. "Lord, I give you my spirit. I commend my spirit to you." Jesus did. "Father, into thy hands I commend my spirit." In that case it meant death. In Stephen's case it meant death; and in your case it will mean death also. Not physical death necessarily, but the death you've been trying to die for so many years. All you need to do is quit trying to nail yourself on a cross, just commend your spirit to Him and that will bring the death that He can change into resurrection. "Therefore we are buried with him by baptism into death: that like as Christ was raised up from the dead by the glory of the Father, even so we also should walk in newness of life" (Rom. 6:4). We die that we might live again.

7.   Forgive and bless. Once, when I was doing a study on forgiveness, I heard myself pray these words about a certain man: "Lord, if he pleases you, he pleases me." That's a heavy prayer. The indication of the prayer is this: "Lord, if he doesn't please you, change him.

But if you're satisfied with how he is, I am too."
How do we get to that? We begin by being filled
with the Spirit. And then each of these
steps—take them with you, think about them,
study them—will help you to recognize that
mercy is what you must live on.

After a great negative experience in my life, I
was deeply wounded by a woman and I
couldn't get the thing straightened out. In fact,
she came to me in private asking my
forgiveness but then she said to me, "If anyone
asks me, I will not tell the truth." She had
started a rumor which had gone all through the
church. She continued, "I will never come back
to the church because I am embarrassed and if
anyone asks me if it was a lie, I will never tell
them, but I'm asking you to forgive me."

I got in my car and I said, "God, this isn't fair.
She asked for my forgiveness so she can get
right with you, but half the people still believe
the lie she started. What am I to do?" The Lord
answered, "I have forgiven you of more than
you have ever been accused."

"Blessed are the merciful for they shall
obtain mercy."

CHAPTER SEVEN

Pure in Heart

BLESSED ARE THE PURE IN HEART:
FOR THEY SHALL SEE GOD. (Matt. 5:8)

Whenever I receive a word from God I must first appropriate it for my life in every way I know how. In that level of my ability before I can preach it, I say, "Lord, let this be a part of my life." And you must do the same, for that's what Jesus taught.

Did you know that Jesus had to learn? The Bible says, "Though he were a Son, yet learned he obedience by the things which he suffered" (Heb. 5:8). We forget that sometimes, don't we? We tend to think that Jesus as a babe was a man to begin with. But He grew from babyhood to manhood. Why? So that we can have a high priest who is touched with the feelings of our infirmities. We don't go through even one thing He hasn't gone through before us. That's why we can trust Him in prayer. We say, "Lord, you understand these feelings. You know what it is to feel this." That becomes very exciting.

"Blessed are the pure in heart for they shall see God." "Pure" comes from a word that means no mixture at all. Nothing added. *Catharos* is the Greek word and it means, "pure, as having been cleansed into perfect cleanliness." Strong word, isn't it? "Blessed are the pure in heart." And that's not the way we talk to one another. The way we talk to one another is to compare with each other. We have a tendency to say, "Well, I know how you feel because everybody feels that way at one time or another." We can fake it; we can talk like we're pure inside when we aren't. True purity comes as we are poor in spirit—humbly recognizing and mourning for our sin. Then Jesus can forgive us and teach us how to walk purely with Him. That takes meekness.

Another word for meek is "teachable." Being teachable is important to being pure in heart. Unfortunately, a lot of us are teachable only in certain areas, or if it involves the right teacher. Meekness says, "I don't care who the teacher is." It comes from a spiritual hunger, that gnawing inside, the craving that nothing—not natural food, not love in the natural, not sex, nor things—can satisfy. We're driven. We need someone just to say, "You know what your problem is? You're hungry for God." And until God meets that hunger we'll go on collecting things, constantly reaching for another experience, changing homes, etc. All this will be in an effort to try to satisfy what can only be satisfied by Him. Mercifulness follows that. We can't be merciful before we come this way. It's a progressive thing.

Paul said, "Forgetting those things which are behind, and reaching forth unto those things which are before I press toward the mark for the prize of the high calling of God" (Phil. 3:13-14).

Forgetting what I'm not—I now have a new goal which I shall become and I am reaching toward. For God to give me revelation is often nearly devastating for me, seeing what I am supposed to be and what I am. This has made me want to leave the ministry innumerable times as the Word came alive to me. But the Lord said, "Back on the job!"

"I can't; I'm not here."

He says, "I know, but you're not there either any more."

Do these things happen automatically in your spiritual growth? No, it depends on how we read the Word. The Bible can either be read as law or principles. Any book can.

I wrote a book for singles, divorcees and

widows. People from time to time read my book looking for a formula of *How to Be Happy in No Man's Land*. I wrote this to help unmarried women learn that they can feel complete and have happiness while remaining unmarried. That was my goal. Many of God's people read that book looking for law. They're trying to find the formula. Some people pull out what they think is a formula: "If you do this and this and don't do that, you will be happy." So they do the do's and don't the don'ts, and become unhappy. Then they're mad at me.

I didn't write a book of formula or law. The Old Testament was a book of law. Nobody could keep it so nobody found happiness until Jesus came. He said, "I can and I will." And He did. He kept it. Then He stood up and dared to say, "All right, I didn't come to set that law aside, I've come to *be* it. I have fulfilled the law. Now I give you a new commandment. I bring you the New Testament. This cup is the New Testament in my blood." That's what we call the Lord's Supper. What does this mean? It means that I have access to becoming everything Jesus became as I appropriate the truth.

I preach things that amaze me. You'll laugh at this but you can go back through my itinerary and check with the pastors—I have been known often to answer my own altar calls. I'm not the authority over what I'm saying; I'm

God's servant. You will find God is going to teach you so much while you're sharing with others. And you'll think, "Oh, that will fit! I can't wait to get out of here to appropriate that to my life." Where does it all start? We point to our hearts because we don't know how else to point to our innermost beings.

The word "heart" refers to the seat of so many things. Scripturally, in the New Testament alone the heart is spoken of as the seat of physical life, moral nature and spiritual life, grief, joy, desires, affections, perceptions, thoughts, understanding, reasoning powers, imagination, conscience, intentions, purposes, will and faith. It is spoken of as the seat of one's intellect, emotions and innermost being. We're dealing with the heart, and with attitudes. Attitudes stem from the heart, not the mind only. It's not just will power, but it involves a change of all the inward parts. The inward man is renewed daily. Paul said it that way in 2 Cor. 4:16. The inside man is being renewed.

The Bible says, "Beholding Him as in a glass" (2 Cor. 3:18). The word translated "glass" means "mirror." We are changed or likened into the same image from glory to glory.

When I look at Him, when His Word comes forth from me, I'm being changed. The Word is the mirror. This is typified by the laver of the tabernacle when the priest would see his own reflection in the water.

What does it mean to be pure in heart? A pure heart, with nothing added. How do you get that way? *By being cleansed.* "Now the end of the commandment is charity out of a *pure heart,* and of a good conscience and of faith unfeigned" (1 Tim. 1:5). "Holding the mystery of the faith in a *pure conscience*" (1 Tim. 3:9). "I thank God, whom I serve from my forefathers with *pure conscience,* that without ceasing I have remembrance of thee in my prayers night and day" (2 Tim. 1:3). "*Unto the pure all things are pure:* but unto them that are defiled and unbelieving is nothing pure; but even their mind and conscience is defiled" (Titus 1:15). "Let us draw near with a *true heart* in full assurance of faith having our hearts sprinkled from an evil conscience and our bodies washed with pure water" (Heb. 10:22).

What do each of these verses tell us? They reveal that from Him purity is received. "I am meek and lowly of heart. And what I am ye shall be also. Where I am, what I am, who I am—greater things than I do shall ye do. Father, the glory that thou hast given me I have given them." Blessed assurance that what Jesus is we can be also. It is Christ in us!

We live far beneath our privileges of being holy as He is holy. Inward purity comes from receiving Him within. I think you've discovered by now that most of us have a problem with impurity. I'm not talking only about filthy minds or X-rated dreams or thievery. But we manipulate people, don't we? We have something to gain by most of what we do. I was talking with someone recently and he said, "You know, God has been dealing with me for a period of time—with the Jacob nature in me. The ability to get my own way causes me to approach life like a chess game. I can see six moves ahead. If I say this to them, and they do this to that and they jump there, I'll have what I want."

Women are fabulous manipulators by nature. We're second only to kids. We have an ability to manipulate, to set the pace of a whole day and not say one bad thing. But God is dealing with that in us. Why? It does not fit in with purity. And that's what He's bringing us into—inward purity. God first showed me this, when He said, "I ought to call you Jacob."

I responded, "Please don't call me Jacob—call me Israel. Lord, change the Jacob nature that's there. I don't know how you're going to do it, but I'll do my part."

Don't ever make that prayer unless you're ready, because the Holy Spirit will say, "I hear that prayer." Ever since then, every time I start to connive, the Holy Spirit says, "One question, why are you doing this?" I have to back up eight moves to find out my true motives and I never like it when I get there.

I can rationalize it away, because there is always something good in everything I do. I can say, "Lord, the reason I'm doing this is that in so doing I will bless these and those and I will bring glory to your name."

He is always faithful to remind me: "Keep going. You've got two more jumps."

"Yes, Lord, it is true and please don't stop wrestling with me." He will always win, but it sometimes takes longer than I think it should.

I believe the day of saying one thing and living another is ending. We've had it. The church now knows we've had it. We've had impure motivations, etc. I believe that the clean-up program is on.

"Judgment must begin," the Bible says, "at the house of God" (1 Pet. 4:17). I think judgment has begun. Some of you are going to be deeply hurt as a result of this because you're going to learn some things about some leaders that you have on a pedestal right now. It's going to hurt you. There will be some exposures, and I pray to God that they won't come from the body of Christ.

When God wants to expose something, don't allow yourself to become a part of that exposure. When God wants to reveal it, He'll do it without your help. If He has your help He will expose it and then judge you. That's the fairness of our God.

So if some leaders you hold in very high esteem are exposed in certain areas of their lives, don't allow yourself to believe that you're doing the right thing by uncovering a brother. When these people fall, God's going to pick them up again and He's going to bless them and heal them, and use them in a whole new dimension that they've never known before. That's our Lord. So when they fall, just pray and bless them, because God's going to have a church with inward purity.

The world has looked on us and said, "Hypocrisy rules in the church." Frankly, they haven't been too far off base. But it's changing. I'm not getting by with what I used to. You're not getting by with what you used to. God points to something in my life and says, "That's over!"

I say, "Are you kidding? I've done it that way for forty-five years."

He answers, "I know it, but now that's over."

"But I used to get by with it and have your blessing."

He answers, "I am aware of that because then you couldn't handle the correction, but now you can."

He is cleansing His church. That's what He's doing. Why? Because He loves us. Because during all those years, every time I won, I really lost. Every time I manipulated people and things to get me in a winning position, I was the loser. I hated myself for years, though I didn't show it by the way I lived. People would say, "Oh, she's so happy!" Then I would go home and look in the mirror and say, "I hate you." But I came across the Scripture, "Thou shalt love thy neighbor as thyself" and then I saw it.

I said, "Lord, I don't know how to like myself. I know me too well." He said, "I'll take care of that."

And, of course, I'm still not what I want to be, but I'm so grateful that I'm not what I once was. I can see changes taking place and that's very exciting to me. I can't take the credit for one change in my life. Not even for the desire to change. That came from Him too. "To God be the glory, great things He hath done." That's my whole song. No wonder I praise Him. I'm a living miracle of His love and grace. *And so are you!*

When you really know that, when you really submit to the Lord, it's thrilling. "Commit thy way unto the Lord; trust also in him; and he shall bring it to pass" (Ps. 37:5). We need to learn what the Hebrew word "commit" means. It is a lover's term and the word means "wallow." The indication is that just as a woman totally submits and wallows in her husband's love we should do the same with the Lord. This kind of trust means not being fearful of being hurt or taken advantage of. That's the term that's used there. Just commit yourself to your Lover.

Gentlemen, you who have wives who trust you that way and just love to be in your arms, now you can understand how much your heavenly Father enjoys that same level of commitment from you. "Do unto me as thou wilt, Lord, because I know you're out to do me good."

"Commit thy way"—it means your way of living unto the Lord. That's bringing you into inward purity. But a second way is by purging or pruning. In fact, the same word is used in this Scripture: "Every branch in me that beareth not fruit, he taketh away: and every branch that beareth fruit, He purgeth" (John 15:2). You see, all the dealings of God are not results of negative behavior or wrong attitudes. They are to dig us deep and dig us wide, to increase our capacity for Him.

Have you ever met someone whom you would describe like this? "He's very nice, but he's a very little person." Now we're not speaking of that person's stature but we're talking about the individual knowing very little about life. Such a person has a little world; he lives within a little circle or framework of family and friends and job and he can only talk about

three things: family, friends and job. So we
speak of them as little people. They're nice, but
they're just little people.

We also discover littleness in our concepts of
the family of God. God has allowed babies to be
nourished and cared for sufficiently so as to
become mature adults. That maturity should
not sever us from the awareness and
appreciation of the total family but rather
regulate our thoughts to our position of
responsibility. For too long many of us have
seen ourselves, our church, our denomination
as separate entities unto themselves. In this
day, God is purposing to restore the whole
church. His methods in achieving this are
purging and pruning.

There's pain in purging. Here I am,
branching out, doing a great job and being very
fruitful and along comes the Holy Spirit, and
off goes the branch. "But that was my most
useful branch! Lord, I was best at that."

"I know; wait until you see the new one."

We ask, "Where?" It seems like it will never
happen. But when that new branch comes
forth and the fruit of the Spirit of God comes
forth instead of the abilities of Iverna, people
begin to pluck and eat from it, and they are
nourished and replenished and I stand back
and say, "Oh, God, thank you for not listening
to me when I screamed, 'Ouch!' "

The third way is to absolutely refuse to permit yourself the luxury of insincerity. Our society inadvertently trains us to be beautiful liars. I say, "How do you like my dress?" There wouldn't be one in ten who would say, "I don't like it; it's baggy." Even if all ten thought it.

Some might even say, "You look lovely in it." How can we maintain our sense of integrity and purity of heart while preventing either of these two extremes? Perhaps we could say, "That's a lovely flower on it"—"If there be *any* virtue or *any* praise"—think on that. Philippians 4:9 would be our guideline for this. Honesty and integrity must be coupled with love in order to be Christian.

We even teach our children to lie. Did you know that? I was holding a meeting at a conference ground and they had a staff meeting for one of the members. They invited me to come after the service. A little four-year-old toddler had a birthday that day and a staff member had been given a little bank of a funny character as a joke. When he found out that the little girl had a birthday, he wrapped it up and put a ribbon on it and called her over standing her on a bench. She was very embarrassed. Everybody began to sing, "Happy Birthday," and then he gave her the present. She opened the gift, looked at it and ran down off the bench to her mother who was sitting right next to me. The mother said, "You forgot to say thank you."

The little girl set it down and said, "I don't want it!" Her very embarrassed mother said, "Well, go tell the man, 'Thank you.' "

The little girl looked at her mother and said, "I don't want to because I don't want it!"

So the mother turned over to the man who had given her this and said, "Thank you very much." She then took the gift and told the girl to hold it. And the little girl said, "I don't want to hold it; I don't like it." By now, she was getting very loud. The people, realizing it was a bank, thought it would be nice to come over and put pennies in it. They would come over and ask the girl where the bank was. She would say, "I don't have a bank. My bank is home."

Her mother looked at me with frustration and I said, "This is the most beautiful display of honesty I have seen in years. The child doesn't like the bank and she has dared to say so."

What is omitted from this story is love. The Bible declares we must "speak the truth in love." A child is unprepared for such a balance and is often seen or heard displaying great love (when they are pleased) or speaking the blunt truth. The adult recognizes the need of concern for others while maintaining a walk of integrity before God. Hence, an adult's response to the above might have been, "What a lovely gesture you've made in remembering my birthday." All too often in the area of purity we become entangled again with the yoke of bondage (Gal. 5:1).

The letter of the law such as the little girl was stating was that she honestly did not like the gift. The intention (or spirit) of the law would not demand her to state that she did but rather that she appreciated receiving a gift.

God is going to bring an awareness to us of what it means to speak the truth in love. "I will appropriate this to my life. I refuse to have impurities contaminate the purity that God has brought within my heart." That should be our position. The only part of this thing I can do is to refuse any mixture.

At a meeting where I was the main speaker, a musical group preceded me. They were horrid—not anointed and not good. As soon as they finished, I was introduced and instead of just getting up and starting in the Word, I said, "My, how we appreciated this group, didn't we?"

The Holy Spirit said to me, "You liar!" Now what was I to do with that? I suffered. To make it worse, a minister friend of mine who was there to hear me speak had made arrangements to take me out to dinner afterwards with his wife and family.

When I left the platform and came out, he

said to me, "I thought you'd gotten over lying?"

I said, "Shut up. I don't want to hear it."

When we got to the restaurant he said, "I only have one question and then I promise to let you enjoy your dinner. Why did you have to say anything?"

I answered, "Because my name is Jacob. And I was doing all the right things."

You just can't do all the right things. There is an impurity that comes from being something on the outside that is different from what we are on the inside. This is a far more subtle thing then sexual impurity, etc. It's true of the clergy. It's true of teachers, laymen and counselors. But there is a longing in the heart which cries, "God, make me pure." Why? Is that a matter of pride? The devil will suggest it to you. When the devil talks to me I say, "I'm so glad Jesus told me about you. I'll tell you why. Because I'm in love with Him and I want Him to be proud of me. I really do. I want Him to be able to look down like He did at Job and say, 'Have you considered my servant, Iverna? She loves me, she loves me enough to live my life.' " Now I know I'm not there because I can still see *me*. But I'm getting there because He's changing me. What's the promise to me if I get there? *I shall see God.*

What are *you* looking at? "Oh, I've got so many problems." That's what you see and that's what you're full of. "The light of the body is the eye."

Remember when it was revealed to Elisha where the enemy was and he reported to the king when they were going to have the battle (2 Kings 6:8-17)? Pretty soon the leak got out and the enemy said, "We know who's the head of this problem. His name is Elisha; he's the man of God. Well, go get him!"

And so out came the warriors. The king's very best mighty men were sent forth and they came to the hill where Elisha stayed and they knew he was going to be there. They surrounded the whole area. Elisha had a young servant who was with him, who, upon arising early, saw the peril of being encompassed by the enemy. He cried out to Elisha in fear. But Elisha reassured him, "Don't be afraid!"

"Are you kidding? Don't you see all our enemies?" Elisha was calm because he was looking at the great host of warriors and chariots of the Lord which the servant didn't see.

Have you ever talked to anyone who experienced the same kind of thing? You saw God in the situation but they saw the circumstances. You saw God bringing something to pass and they saw the devil bringing something to pass. They nervously ordered, "Cast it out, do something."

You quietly answered, "Isn't this

wonderful?"

Perhaps that's why there is a scriptural question, "What fellowship hath light with darkness?" Of course, there is no fellowship, but there is always an overtaking. One always overtakes the other. The flip of a switch and darkness leaves. The flip of a switch and darkness returns. It depends on whether you're on or off. If you are light, you don't fellowship with darkness. You *overtake* darkness by the presence of light within you.

Elisha knew the situation. He knew his servant was having a heart attack because he didn't have a spiritual vision. He hadn't learned to see God in things present. He knew miracles had taken place. He believed in God and he probably believed that there would be a God in his future, because Elijah, Elisha's master, had seen a chariot and had been swept away. He had good faith concepts but he didn't have good faith appropriation. So Elisha prayed a simple prayer: "Lord, open his eyes that he may see." And the Bible says that his eyes were opened and he saw the army of the Lord.

That's why I want to come into purity. I want to see you and, when I look at you, to see only Jesus. I want to see God in things present. Every circumstance I come into, every situation in which I'm engaged or involved in any way, I want to know God's in it. It may take me a little longer to find out, but if I know He's there, I'm at peace. "Lord, I know you're in this thing. And I know you're in it to bring good to my life, not only to the others." In the Word God used every situation to benefit His people. Whether it meant taking them into captivity for a period of time that they might come out to true liberty or whether it meant to persecute them so they'd spread the gospel throughout all the earth, it didn't matter. Neither did it matter if they didn't understand at the time it was happening. He understood because His ways are not our ways.

If you have a longing to seek God and know Him as He is, then you have a longing for inward purity, that your inward parts might respond to and be possessed by God.

The person possessed by God becomes His glory revealed to others. Our living, works, and words become God-controlled.

"A word fitly spoken is like apples of gold in pictures of silver" (Prov. 25:11). A single sentence you say may do more than an hour-long message, if it's said under the inspiration of the Holy Spirit in God's time to the person God gave ears to hear it. And if your heart is pure, so is your conversation.

"Unto the pure all things are pure." "I wonder why they said that?" "I wonder why so and so gave this to me?" "I wonder why they asked me to speak?" Have you ever been guilty of asking similar questions? I have. You see, I'm judging them based on me. I'm really revealing myself by my lack of trust for the other person. But that's not evidence of a pure heart. A pure heart is an unmixed heart. The Bible says that God will deal with the pure in purity. *He will deal with the pure in purity.* Do you want to pitch your stubbornness against God? I promise you that He will always win.

God says, "Blessed are the pure in heart for they shall see God. They shall know me and they shall know my ways and I will make my face to shine upon them and I will grant unto them my peace." Is that the cry of your heart?

Father, I ask you to remove all the fear from the reader who would worry about what your purging might mean. And let them have such a hungering and thirsting spirit after purity that there would be no cost too great for them. Amen.

CHAPTER EIGHT

Peacemaking

BLESSED ARE THE PEACEMAKERS:
FOR THEY SHALL BE CALLED THE
CHILDREN OF GOD. (Matt. 5:9)

The Greek word for "peacemaker" is *eirene*.
It means "to set at one again." Our idea of
peacemaking is to discover the problems
involving both sides in a conflict and to try to
determine who owes the apology. In fact, if
we're the third party in a dispute that's exactly
what we do.

We'll never become peacemakers as long as
we are concerned with who is right. That's the
job of a judge. Would you like to be a judge? If
you judge, you shall be judged. That's why I
don't want to judge anything or anyone. I don't
judge you; you don't judge me. Let's let the
Master do it all. But peacemaking differs from
judging in that peacemaking has one goal, one
desire—whatever it takes we've got to get back

together.

Let's say that I approach a friend one morning and say, "Hi there!" And he drags out a hello.

And I say, "Aren't you feeling well?"

He says, "I'm feeling fine." It doesn't take me long to know we're in trouble. I can choose between two alternatives. I can think, "I have done nothing to hurt him. I know my motives have been pure. And if he's got his feelings hurt, he can just sit on them." Now I can take that attitude.

On the other hand, I can have such an absolute determination to set it at one again that I say, "Brother, I don't know what I've done but I ask you to forgive me." Now, how can he fight that? You know, you can fight anything but love. And if my total desire is to set it at one again, that is the beginning of true peacemaking.

But please remember the preceding Beatitudes. We cannot jump from step one to seven. The others have to become attributes given to us by God and become alive within us first in order to keep from being false in our peacemaking. I can say those same words and they will be as sounding brass. We have people who say all the right words, yet their goal is to get the thing out on the table. That's not what a peacemaker does. A peacemaker says, "I want to get this thing together." Well, what's supposed to come together? First of all, the reconciliation of the relationship between people. We have to be related in the right way in life. God has an order for everything. We need to be rightly related with life in every area. God is getting His church back into a position of being rightly related to everything about us. That's when peace will really take over.

We've got to have peace in our minds. A person filled with turmoil very often endeavors to be a peacemaker and instead, he becomes a busybody. Have you ever seen a person like that? Just running around, concerned about everything and his mind is just filled with turmoil and he's always rushing about trying to get this person with that person and that's not what a peacemaker is. That's a busybody.

We can talk to people. We can become "Bibles wired for sound." We can quote verses, and it will all come across like sounding brass. But if you can say, "Sir, I understand what it's like to be filled with confusion and conflict, because I've been there. I know what it is to lay my head on the pillow and realize I ought not to be concerned for the morrow and be filled with the concerns for tomorrow. But, you see, I found a pattern in the Word of God. I found a principle and instead of just ejecting thoughts of concern and worry I became aware that they must be replaced." You can't just not think about a thing. In order not to think about a thing you must have another source of input. And the Bible tells us what to think about. "Whatsoever things are true, honest, just . . ."—and the sum total is—"if there be any virtue"—if you could think of anything that's praiseworthy—"concentrate on it. Think on these things." It really beats counting sheep.

When we begin to see these things, then we're ready to begin to minister to others because we've learned the means of appropriation. Then we will have an understanding of God and ourselves. And the reason I did that backwards for you is because many people don't realize that it's our self-love that brings us to the Lord. Why did you want to come to the Lord?

"Lord, I come just as I am. . . ." He sets us at one with himself. Can you imagine the fellowship God had in the garden of Eden? Do you know that God has been seeking that same kind of fellowship all through the ages? It is His desire to set us at one again with Him. We need to learn how to just love Him. One of the great things that is being taught today is the ability to communicate. Not just talking but learning to commune with one another. It's good and we need to learn this.

God is doing something about this. Some

parents have a problem with communication with their children. If I would put you in a room with your child and turn off the television and the radio and provide nothing external for you to do, you might just look at your child. He might look at you and say, "How have you been?"

"Oh, really good. Things going well at school?"

"Yes, really well. How were things at home today?"

"Oh, fine."

Now what's wrong with that? We haven't learned to be at peace with one another. I have a friend with whom I can sit for hours and never talk. We just fellowship. That's delightful. I haven't always had that. I appreciate her so much. She's my companion and secretary.

That's what God wants us all to come into. Where you're not always having to say, "Lord, forgive me." "Lord, do this." Instead, you just say, "Oh, Lord, it's so good to be with you. I just love you." I'm on the road so much, and I'm often alone. Motel rooms become my home, and I've learned to make it work for me. I carry little artificial flowers with me, etc. I create a setting and I say, "Welcome home, Iverna." I almost never feel alone. If you would see me in my room, you would probably commit me to some institution, because I small-talk with the

Lord like this: "Lord, this is a nice room. Thanks for providing it. I'm so glad you're here with me. I love you." Such a conversation is not one way for I have a great sense of His presence which communicates His love back to me.

You have only one thing to communicate to your unsaved children and that's love. We need to be interested in everyone being properly related to God. And then and only then can I experience the kind of peacemaking Jesus describes. We have to come to this place. I believe the church of the Lord Jesus Christ has to come together.

"Great peace have they which love thy law: and nothing shall offend them" (Ps. 119:165). What do we get for being peacemakers? "They shall be called the children of God." I want you to realize the steps of progression that are bringing you into sonship. When I get to the place when I can say, "All I want to know, my brother, is do you know the Father? Do you know Jesus?"—that's maturity. Every time the Holy Spirit flows through us, a little bit of us flows out. That means we're being cleansed. Less of us and more of Him. But if we try to clog it up until we're pure, then we will have to be broken. "Get under the spout where the glory comes out."

We've already alluded to the fact that some

of us have had an idea about Christianity—that it was an immunity program. We thought if we accepted the Lord Jesus Christ we would be automatically immune to all problems and trials and afflictions and everything would suddenly be a garden of roses and there would be nothing left to bother us. It didn't take very long after we met the Lord for us to see that we really had little concept of what it meant to be a Christian. And long ago we've passed steps one and two. We've come into this—"I need thee, oh, I need thee. I'm sorry for my sin; be merciful to me." Finally we progress along until we're saying, "Teach me thy ways. Show me thy ways, O God."

There is a big difference between the acts of God and the ways of God. The acts of God are what we see—evidence we have before us. He heals the sick, etc. They are the acts of God and they are of God and they are beautiful. But that's all the children of Israel were willing to see, wasn't it? So the Bible tells us that He let them see His acts, but He made known His ways only unto Moses. I want Him to show me His ways. I want to be God-controlled. I want to understand the concepts of God—who He is and His ways.

My children—my daughter, son-in-law, and my son—know me very well. If you were to pick up the phone today and call California and say,

"Do you know what your mom did?" They would know by what you said whether or not I was guilty. That's because they know me. Most of the time they probably would say, "I believe it!" But if you told them something that was totally unlike me, any one of the three of them would say, "I don't believe that, because I know her." That is just one minute reason for us to learn the ways of God.

I meet people everywhere who tell me what God did to them. They blame so many things on Him. I always say, "I'm glad you told me that because I can straighten you out. I know Him personally; He would never do that!" Then I reveal the true God to them.

I want to know His ways for so many reasons. And because of that I have a hunger and a thirst after things that are upright and fair. I hate things that are not fair. That's why I have such a strong response to any form of prejudice. It is so unfair—to be judged on the basis of someone's prejudice. That doesn't even give me a chance. It doesn't give you a chance either.

I learned I have to be merciful because I live on mercy. Every relationship I have with Him is based on His mercy, not on my goodness. Therefore, it's not hard for me. I have people say to me, "You know, it's amazing how you can forgive people."

I reply, "Don't be amazed; that's not because I'm so good; it's because I'm so needy. I need so much mercy that I have to give mercy."

We must have a singleness of heart and purpose: that I may please Him by knowing my heart and remembering that the Bible says, "The heart is deceitful and desperately wicked." But the next verse says, "I the Lord search the heart, I try the reins" (Jer. 17:9). He can know our hearts. Daily, I say a prayer: "Lord, let everyone I come in contact with be blessed because of you in me. And cause my life to please you this day, no matter what the day brings." When I pray that, I am really praying, "Let the words of my mouth, and the meditation of my heart, be acceptable in thy sight, O Lord, my strength, and my redeemer" (Ps. 19:14). I trust you've come to that position in your life too.

Maybe you'll always understand peacemaking if you add three words to it.

AT ANY COST. Not *peace* at any cost. *Peacemaking* at any cost. Peace at any cost demands compromise. I don't believe that is always the position of a Christian. But peacemaking doesn't demand that. Peacemaking demands everything. It demands you give everything.

CHAPTER NINE

Persecution

BLESSED ARE THEY WHICH ARE
PERSECUTED FOR RIGHTEOUSNESS'
SAKE: FOR THEIRS IS THE KINGDOM
OF HEAVEN. (Matt. 5:10-11)

"Blessed are ye—in an enviable position,
joyful, glad, happy." All of those words are
proper descriptions or definitions of the word
"blessed." To be envied. In a happy state.
Someone has said happiness is related to
happenings; joy is not. They are correct, in
fact. But in the way this word is used they are
not right. Because this is not talking about
happenings. Children will be happy on
Christmas, because of the happenings—they
get presents, etc., but it's a sad thing when
adults relate their happiness to that too.

Here we're talking about a state of blissful
dwelling when we say "happy" or "to be
envied." The person who is persecuted is to be
envied. Now this word "persecute" means "to

pursue." Very few of us have been literally pursued. We've had words spoken against us. We've been ridiculed in certain circles. We were made fun of because it is not always popular to speak in tongues. I grew up in a church that practiced glossalalia, so we knew what it was to see the tomatoes hit the windows—from the ones who were making fun of us on the outside. We were called the "holy rollers." I thought that was real persecution.

We really don't know much about persecution because the word is so strong in the original language. The best way to describe it would be if somebody made up his mind to attack someone else and said, "I'm going to get you!"

We have seen this in the politics of our country. We've seen literal persecution. The Word says, "You're in an enviable state if you're being pursued for my sake." Don't ever pull little bits and pieces out of the whole of the Scripture. It is not a joyful position to be in when somebody says, "'I'm out to kill you" when it isn't for God's sake—if it's just a personal thing.

I wonder if any of us have enough of God in us to be worth being persecuted. I wonder if any of us are an actual threat to hell. But we're becoming that, because for the first time in many years the church is waking up to who she

is. The individuals who make up the church of
the Lord Jesus Christ are beginning to become
aware that one little tiny widow woman who
really has come to an understanding of who she
is in Christ can cause all hell to quake when she
hits her knees.

For years we didn't know that. I can just see
the enemy saying, "Oh, leave them alone;
they'll destroy themselves." It's only been
during the last twenty years that we've given
him any reason to be threatened by us. Finally,
we're coming together and that's threatening
to the enemy.

We're coming together, and there is a
persecution that's just beginning. That word
"pursue" speaks to us of *diabolos* which means
to accuse. Thirty-four times in Scripture that
same word is used of Satan. He is the accuser of
the brethren. Satan is not out to get you as a
person. He has one goal—to usurp worship
from God to himself. For a long time the
church merely went through the procedures of
"churchianity" ("let them do their thing; let
them be religious"). But fifteen years or so ago
men all over the world began to rise up and say,
"Let's just praise the Lord." It hit in your
church and in my church. We began to hear
this teaching from our priests and rabbis and
pastors and shepherds and leaders and so on.
We started to hear these truths come to us—we

are the people of the Lord; we were created to praise Him. When that happened, the body of Christ began to come together.

At one conference I attended in Israel I sat between a Jewess and an Arab. We couldn't communicate, except by smiling back and forth at each other. But we stood and sang "Hallelujah" in every language of the world. I tell you it was the most moving experience I have ever had in my life. We couldn't talk, but when we got together we could raise our hands and sing, "Hallelujah."

The enemy now has a reason to be threatened, for the church is coming together. Not in one building or a single denomination. We're coming together in doctrine, in truth. What is the truth? "Let's just praise the Lord." And you're going to hear more about praise and worship than you've heard before since praise is a stepping stone to worship.

Because of that there will be persecution. Please understand me when I tell you that Satan is on a chain. When Jesus came forth from the dead, He jingled two keys. He came through the domain of Satan victorious over hell and death. He said, "Look, Satan, I've got them!" And no longer does Satan have the ability to kill the people of God. Death was taken out of his control. No longer can the grave be a frightening scene for those who know Jesus because it's a time of graduation; it's not death. There's victory. The only power Satan has toward the believer is that dirty power of deception and we're stupid enough to listen to him. Jesus said, "Satan is the father of lies!" (John 8:44).

Satan's pursuit of us is involved in a much higher goal than the destruction of one person. His war is with God and his goal is to displace Him on the throne.

Let me share a statement made by a Detroit pastor. "Society and church demand conformity. If you fall beneath their standards they will punish you. If you rise above their standards they will persecute you." Many of us have suffered the persecution that hurts the very most. This is not the persecution from Satan, but from the brothers and the sisters. "Those who go into the house of the Lord with me," David said, "they're the ones." Church, I have bad news for you and good news. First the bad. Persecution has just begun. We're going to see brothers and sisters in the church who are setting down absolutes: this is the way to worship, this is how we do it, this is the law. And if you fall beneath that standard or rise above it, either one becomes a threat to their structures.

Spiritual hunger overtakes you, a decision will have to be made. Will you worship man's way as the priests did in Ezekiel 44, taking that compromise position of keeping everyone happy, or will you identify with the sons of Zadok who would permit no compromise? "Zadok" means "righteous" and the righteous can be satisfied with nothing less than the ways of the Lord. It is human nature to want to be both understood and accepted and I have no doubt that the prophets, priests, and kings of the Bible all faced the dilemma of pleasing men or God. Yet, it's plain to see that the blessing of peace, prosperity, and power was given to those whose ways pleased the Lord.

In light of one of the meanings for the word "persecution," which is "to be pursued," we experience such persecution as God pursues us.

Have you ever read the poem called "The Hound of Heaven"? It speaks of God's pursuit after you. Did you ever try to get rid of Him or to shake Him off your trail? "God, now I'm going in this place."

"It's not a place where you ought to be. How come you're going there?" The "Hound of Heaven" was after me. He said, "Blessed are you if I'm pursuing you."

It didn't feel good until I turned around and said, "All right, I give up!"

In response, He said, "Good, I've been waiting for this for forty-three years." He reached down, picked me up, put me in His bosom and said, "From now on we are a team." And where He goes, I go.

Now, can you see how blessed I was? There are some people who have never known that kind of drawing from God. There are men and women today who would give anything to hunger after spiritual things. There are men and women today who would give anything to have enough of God in them just to be threatening to hell.

Do you understand that the world has little righteousness left? How many of you think you could get a fair shake in court? How much righteousness is there? It would be a tragedy if we could take a poll to discover how many people cheat in life, cheat on income tax and other matters. We scream if we get short-changed but we smile if we get change for a ten when we paid only five. No righteousness, and yet there is a thirst for righteousness, isn't there? We read stories where men in the past just gave their word and it was a sealed thing for life. They would never violate their oath. In the present day, however, the unjust are becoming more unjust still. We sign on dotted line after dotted line and still have no guarantee.

Do you think you're not going to be persecuted for being righteous? Sure you are. He says, "You are finding my kingdom, right now, because you're making me king and you're standing in honor. You're a royal nation." Royalty cannot approach things in the same manner as commoners. We are learning that one thing royalty must do is to live in constant protection of the throne. That's why we walk around saying, "Yes, there are negatives, but I'm a child of the King and my King ultimately wishes good for me. And all He's doing in my life right now is preparing me to rule and reign with Him."

In Hebrews 11, there is a beautiful listing of the heroes of faith. Verses 33-39 describe some of their persecutions. These are far greater than anything we have experienced. The physical mistreatment is described but the mental tortures and perplexities are left to our imagination. The one characteristic which is evident in each of them is faith. "These all died in the faith not having received the promise." Those of us who have received the promise of our Lord Jesus Christ should not only suffer the persecution in faith but also acknowledge the counsel of St. Paul—"In everything give thanks for this is the will of God in Christ Jesus concerning you."

CHAPTER TEN

Accepting Attitudes

Although we have spoken of these beautiful sayings of Jesus as "attitudes we are to be," we have also attempted to define them as principles of living.

It is natural for us, upon meditation after reading this book, to begin a mental programming which will result in conformity to its contents. We need only reflect on the past to realize the impossibility of this task. As surely as we cannot comprehend the spiritual with the natural mind neither can we build the spiritual man with natural methods.

So often in Scripture we find the word "let" (i.e., "Let this mind be in you which was also in Christ Jesus" [Phil. 2:5]; "Let the word of Christ dwell in you richly" [Col. 3:16]; "Let brotherly love continue" [Heb. 13:1]). It is not in acquiescence to the truth nor in a resolution to adhere to it that kingdom living is discovered. Rather, it is in letting the King rule in every area of our lives and rejoicing in that delightful awareness that "He doeth all things well" which produces righteousness, peace, and joy in the Holy Ghost. As we become better acquainted with the King, we will be less concerned with His kingdom yet, more appreciative of being in it.

Heavenly Father, Creator of all mankind and giver of eternal life through your Son, Jesus Christ, we pray that by your Holy Spirit you will create in us a clean heart and renew a right spirit. Cause us to become sons which please you that we may live in fellowship with the Father, Son, and Holy Spirit. Make us to know thy ways and strengthen us where we are weak. May our wills be so united with your will that every motive and action, every thought and desire, will be an evidence of your glory. Thank you for your Word which speaks hope and life and direction to us. In faith, Father, we ask; in faith we allow; in faith we endure; and in faith we receive our inheritance. We bless and thank you in Jesus' name. Amen.

**If you enjoyed this book may we recommend other best
sellers available where paperbacks are sold or use this order
form:**

Qty.		Price	Total
___	Daughter of Destiny—Kuhlman—Buckingham	$1.95	___
___	Day the Dollar Dies—Cantelon	1.45	___
___	Eldridge Cleaver: Reborn—Oliver	1.95	___
___	Healed of Cancer—Jo Lawson	1.95	___
___	Hustler for the Lord—Larry Jones	1.95	___
___	The Jesus Factor—David Manuel	1.95	___
___	Move That Mountain—Jim Bakker	1.95	___
___	On the Other Side—Ford, Balsiger, Tanner	1.95	___
___	Prison to Praise—Merlin Carothers	1.50	___
___	Run Baby Run—Nicky Cruz	1.50	___
___	Shout It From the Housetops—Pat Robertson	1.95	___
___	The Big 3 Mountain-Movers—Jim Bakker	1.95	___
___	Visions of Jesus—Chet & Lucile Huyssen	1.95	___
	Add 10% *for Shipping*		___
	Total		___

☐ Send Free Order Form—over 250 titles
☐ Send Free Information about *Logos Journal* Magazine
   Include payment to:
      LIF BOOKS
      Box 191
      Plainfield, NJ 07061

Name _____

Address _____

City _____ State _____

                                    Zip_____